Joan of Arc

An Enthralling Guide to a Peasant Girl's Rise in Medieval France and Her Timeless Legacy as a National Heroine

© Copyright 2024 - All rights reserved.

The content contained within this book may not be reproduced, duplicated, or transmitted without direct written permission from the author or the publisher.

Under no circumstances will any blame or legal responsibility be held against the publisher, or author, for any damages, reparation, or monetary loss due to the information contained within this book, either directly or indirectly.

Legal Notice:

This book is copyright protected. It is only for personal use. You cannot amend, distribute, sell, use, quote, or paraphrase any part, or the content within this book, without the consent of the author or publisher.

Disclaimer Notice:

Please note the information contained within this document is for educational and entertainment purposes only. All effort has been executed to present accurate, up-to-date, reliable, and complete information. No warranties of any kind are declared or implied. Readers acknowledge that the author is not engaging in the rendering of legal, financial, medical, or professional advice. The content within this book has been derived from various sources. Please consult a licensed professional before attempting any techniques outlined in this book.

By reading this document, the reader agrees that under no circumstances is the author responsible for any losses, direct or indirect, that are incurred as a result of the use of the information contained within this document, including, but not limited to, errors, omissions, or inaccuracies.

Free limited time bonus

Stop for a moment. We have a free bonus set up for you. The problem is this: we forget 90% of everything that we read after 7 days. Crazy fact, right? Here's the solution: we've created a printable, 1-page pdf summary for this book that you're reading now. All you have to do to get your free pdf summary is to go to the following website: **https://livetolearn.lpages.co/enthrallinghistory/**

Or, Scan the QR code!

Once you do, it will be intuitive. Enjoy, and thank you!

Table of Contents

INTRODUCTION: LA PUCELLE 1
CHAPTER 1 – EARLY VISIONS 5
CHAPTER 2 – A CALL TO ARMS 13
CHAPTER 3 – THE MAIDEN AT ORLÉANS 20
CHAPTER 4 – THE TRIUMPH AT REIMS 30
CHAPTER 5 – THE CAPTURE 36
CHAPTER 6 – TRIAL OF FAITH 41
CHAPTER 7 – MARTYRDOM AND AFTERMATH 49
CHAPTER 8 – SAINTHOOD 58
CHAPTER 9 – A LASTING LEGACY 69
CHAPTER 10 – THE TREATMENT OF OTHER WOMEN WITH VISIONS 82
CONCLUSION 87
HERE'S ANOTHER BOOK BY ENTHRALLING HISTORY THAT YOU MIGHT LIKE 92
FREE LIMITED TIME BONUS 93
BIBLIOGRAPHY 94
IMAGE SOURCES 100

Introduction: La Pucelle

"In Joan of Arc at the age of sixteen there was no promise of romance. She lived in a dull little village on the frontiers of civilization: she had been nowhere and had seen nothing; she knew none but simple shepherd folk; she had never seen a person of note; she hardly knew what a soldier looked like; she had never ridden a horse, nor had a warlike weapon in her hand; she could neither read nor write; she could spin and sew; she knew her catechism and her prayers and the fabulous histories of the saints, and this was all her learning. That was Joan at sixteen."

- Mark Twain, *Personal Recollections of Joan of Arc, by the Sieur Louis de Conte*[1]

History has more than its fair share of war heroes and almost-mythical legends—medieval tales of knights in shining armor who bravely storm castles fighting for king and country—but the famous example of a woman doing the same is rare. Typically, female warriors and tactical heroes are relegated to the background, only to be discovered centuries later by a niche historian searching for the women who *must* have been there all along.

Joan of Arc (also known as Jeanne d'Arc, The Maid, or La Pucelle) is the most famous exception to this rule. She is now known to us as the shining beacon of France. She is a symbol of French resistance and

---

[1] Mark Twain, *Personal Recollections of Joan of Arc, by the Sieur Louis de Conte* (Harper & Brothers, 1896).

enthusiasm, the icon that men have followed into battle for over five hundred years. She is a saint and the protector of France—but at her core, she was an intelligent and brave teenage girl executed before she could see her mission to its bloody end.

The simplicity of Joan's upbringing was steeped in the tumultuous context of the Hundred Years' War, a lengthy conflict between France and England that had ravaged the continent for over a hundred years, as its name suggests. The war began in 1337 after the Black Death swept across Europe and killed almost half of its population, just as tensions were rising in England and France. The feudal system in France was beginning to collapse, in part because of the sudden population decline, and the Knights Templar (a Catholic military order) had been disbanded by Philip VI of France. All this fed the ongoing tensions between England and France surrounding the succession of the French throne.

When Charles IV died from a short illness (possibly pneumonia) in 1328, he left no male heir to succeed to the throne. According to French law at the time, a woman could not inherit the crown, so the title was passed to the king's cousin, who would become King Philip VI. But there was another claimant to the throne. Edward III of England claimed the right to the French throne via his mother, arguing that while a woman could not inherit the throne, there was no reason she could not pass it along to the next male heir. This tension boiled over in 1337 when King Philip VI seized Gascony from the English, spurring Edward III to take his claim by force.

By the time Joan was born, the war had raged in one form or another for seventy-five years, and almost all of northern France was occupied by the English. The quiet village in which Joan was born, Domrémy in the region of Lorraine in eastern France, was close to the fighting, so from a young age, Joan saw firsthand what the ravages of war could be. It can be argued that this is what inspired her to follow her voices into the fray.

In her early life, Joan was educated by her mother in the lessons of Catholicism and the importance of piety. At the age of thirteen, she began to experience angelic visions and to hear the voices of Saint Michael, Saint Catherine, and Saint Margaret. The sound of bells preceded messages from these angels, guiding her destiny, until finally one of these messages changed the course of her life. The message received from her angelic companions called for her to break a great siege at Orléans, drive the English out of France, and clear the way for the Dauphin Charles VII to lay his claim to the French throne.

Guided by the strength of her visions, Joan left her village and began a journey to meet with the Dauphin, marking the beginning of her public mission. She faced some doubts from Charles VII and his advisors but managed to win over the Dauphin with the strength of her conviction. Clad in what would become a distinctive banner and white armor, Joan led the French army to a series of remarkable victories, most notably lifting the siege of Orléans in 1429, paving the way for Charles VII's coronation.

Her success garnered as much ire as admiration, and the English searched for ways to squash this boost to the French army from the beginning of the battle for Orléans. They eventually succeeded in capturing Joan and, after a highly public trial, executed Joan of Arc by burning her at the stake on May 30, 1431.

In three short years, Joan turned the tide of the Hundred Years' War and created a legacy that has lasted for well over five hundred years. Since then, she has become an almost mythical figure, constantly reinterpreted by new philosophical, social, and even psychological movements. Centuries after her martyrdom, Joan of Arc was finally declared a saint—and the patron saint of France, at that—defining her as one of the most popular medieval icons in France and beyond. Her image has been used all over the world as a representation of bravery in the face of the impossible and the power of what a woman can do. Joan of Arc is both a unifying and divisive figure, a feminist icon, and the national symbol of France. Her remarkable life will likely continue to be analyzed and re-examined for centuries to come.

Join us as we learn more about her life and dive into the circumstances surrounding her execution. It is easy to assume you know everything about Joan of Arc, but perhaps you did not know about the political influences on her capture and execution. When you initially learned about Joan of Arc, you may have found out that she was burned for being a witch and that her enemies believed she might have been crazy or blasphemous for hearing voices from "God." It might surprise you to learn that her execution was not as simple as that. There was no "test" of her witchcraft, nor were her accusers unfaithful or atheistic. In fact, her martyrdom happened in a confusing twist of politics and propaganda that may seem eerily familiar if you are a fan of wartime history.

Delving into Joan of Arc's biography provides a rich tapestry of historical events and personal triumphs. Thanks to her well-documented trials, we have a complete view of Joan's life from its beginning to its untimely end. The transcripts of her initial Trial of Faith, its investigation, and the transcript of her posthumous Trial of Nullification were very well preserved, creating an invaluable document for historians today.

Understanding the history around Joan of Arc offers us insight into the complex relationship between religion, politics, and warfare in medieval Europe. Her life exemplifies the power of conviction, and the impact one person can have on the course of history. Her story is not just a tale of military bravery and martyrdom but a testament to the endurance of the human spirit, the conviction of women, and the power of national identity.

The fact that her trials have been so well-preserved has also inspired artists and writers for centuries, reflecting how society changes as time goes on. From Christine de Pizan writing an epic poem celebrating La Pucelle to George Bernard Shaw using her canonization to explore his political views, Joan of Arc has been a vessel for artists to see themselves in the heroine and use her to explore their own artistic ideas.

The depiction of Joan of Arc has changed as history does, as seen in some of the paintings portraying her life. They change from highly feminine portrayals to abstract images exploring her psychology, from emphasizing her femininity to showing the masculine power that coursed through her. While most of this book is devoted to Joan of Arc's life and history, we also take time to explore how her life has become a myth in and of itself and how that myth continues to inspire people into the twenty-first century.

It has now been almost six hundred years since Joan of Arc died, and we are still fascinated by her life. The power of a young woman cannot be ignored, and Joan of Arc exemplifies that in her simple life but multifaceted legacy. In the following pages, we will learn not only about Joan but also about the people who supported the young maiden from Lorraine—the woman who unified France—whose life has not been forgotten in the hundreds of years after her death.

Chapter 1 – Early Visions

Joan of Arc led a remarkable but brief life. Since her death, Joan's legacy has surpassed what that of a typical French peasant girl might have been. She has become renowned for her exceptional military successes and the trial and execution she faced when confronted by her enemies. Where did this sense of courage and piety come from? How would a young girl from the Lorraine region break out and become France's most lasting icon?

Early Years and Family Life

Joan's life began quite simply in the village of Domrémy in the northeastern region of France. Jeanne d'Arc was one of five children born to Jacques d'Arc and Isabelle Romée around 1412. Records of her birth are inaccurate, so we do not know the exact day when she was born. What we do know for sure is that her father was a peasant farmer who took care of about fifty acres of land and supplemented his income as the doyen (elder) of their small village. Joan received an early education that was typical for girls of her time. She helped her father on the farm, learned domestic skills from her mother, and had a deeply religious upbringing in the Catholic faith.

The Hundred Years' War

In the background of this quiet life, the Hundred Years' War raged on. Joan of Arc's life and legend wove itself into the tapestry of the Hundred Years' War, both through her military contributions and in her early life. It would be difficult to explain the entirety of the war here—that would be a whole book in itself—but Joan of Arc's life gives us a glimpse into the many changes that occurred in medieval Europe because of the war.

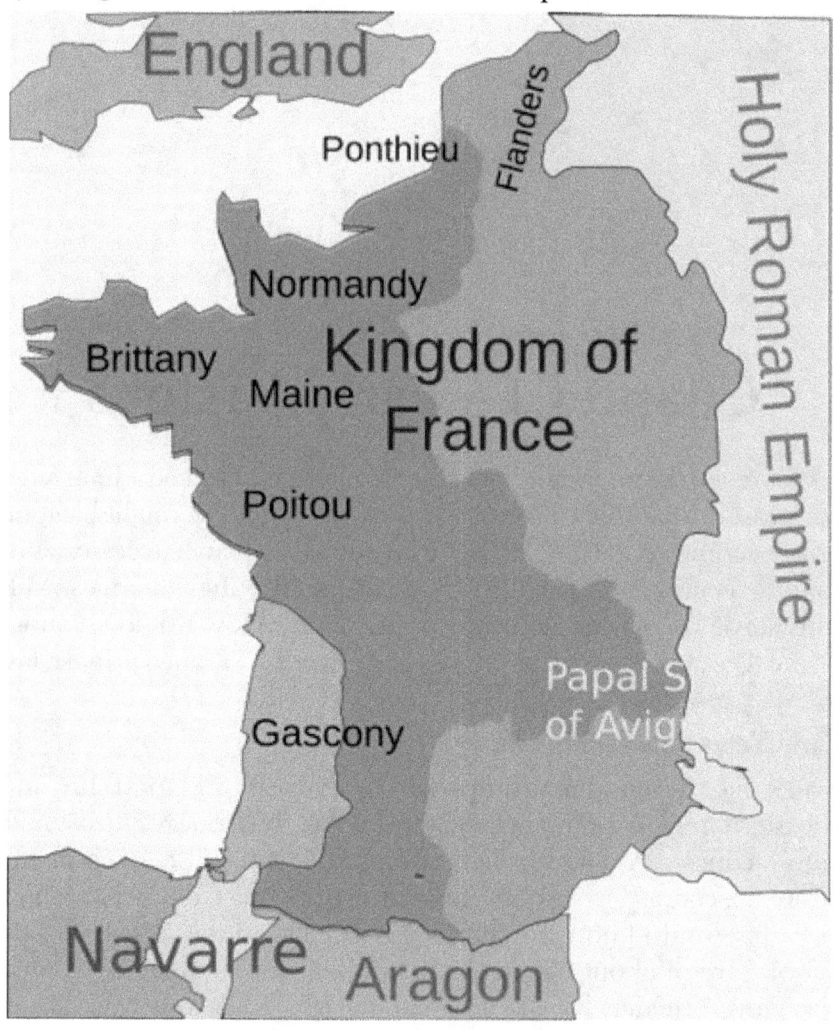

France in 1330. The lighter purple was France before 1214, the darker purple was French acquisitions until 1330, and the pink was England and Guyenne/Gascony in 1330.[1]

Though its name suggests a continuous war, the Hundred Years' War was a collection of conflicts and battles throughout the middle of the fourteenth and fifteenth centuries—spanning over a hundred years and three generations of monarchs—all stemming from a claim to the French throne by the English King, Edward II, in 1337.

Throughout the war, three main factions battled over the territories of France—the English, the Burgundians, and the Armagnacs. The English were led by Edward II (died 1377), Richard II (died 1399), Henry IV (died 1413), Henry V (died 1422), and Henry VI. The French were led by Philip VI (died 1350), John II (died 1364), Charles V (died 1380), Charles VI (died 1422), and finally Charles VII.

The Burgundian faction was smaller, having formed partway through the war after a power struggle with the French (Armagnac). It was led by Philip the Bold (died 1404), John the Fearless (died 1419), and Philip the Good.

At the time of Joan of Arc's life, the English were led by John, Duke of Bedford, in the name of Henry VI, who had been crowned King of England at eight months old when his father died. The French were led by the *Dauphin*, Charles VII, son of the previous king, Charles VI. In France, *Dauphin* was the title bestowed upon the heir to the throne. It was used by Charles VII during his youth when he could not be crowned in the traditional French ceremony at Reims Cathedral.

Reims was in northeast France in a part of the country occupied by English and Burgundian forces. At the time of Joan's life, the English controlled northern France, including Paris, and were advancing on central France via the Loire. The Burgundians and the English controlled Western France, and the French Armagnac faction was tenuously holding on to Central and Southern France. Joan's hometown of Domrémy was on the eastern border of France in an area controlled by the English, though her town was reportedly loyal to the French Crown.

As a result of the Hundred Years' War, the feudal system of medieval Europe began to collapse in France, allowing peasants like Jacques d'Arc to purchase land and work it for themselves. The old system of chivalry was replaced with an organized military, and sentiments of nationalism began to stir in the hearts of French and English citizens, spurred on by figures like Joan. Still, for those who lived between the generations of dukes, kings, and princes fighting for territory, life was a constant struggle for safety and stability, always waiting for the next breakout of war.

Joan's First Visions

According to accounts of her life, Joan was a pious young girl who valued her spiritual connection. There was no indication in her younger life of the military icon she would soon become.

Joan of Arc by Jules Bastien-Lepage.[2]

Her first vision occurred in 1425, when she was about thirteen, in her father's garden. She reportedly saw a blinding light accompanied by a voice, which she later identified as Saint Michael, the Archangel. At first, she was terrified by these strange visions and did not tell anyone about them—not even the village priests who were tasked with her spiritual welfare. As the visions continued, she eventually began to recognize the voices. She claimed they were usually the same three spirits, who would continue to visit her until the day before her death: Saint Michael the Archangel, Saint Catherine, and Saint Margaret. Throughout her life and at trial, Joan maintained that they spoke to her in French.

As time passed, the messages she received grew more complex, until finally, the saints instructed her toward what would eventually become her fate. They told her she needed to aid the Dauphin, Charles VII, in taking France back from the English by leading an army to Orléans and breaking the English siege. The voices also commanded her to drive the English army out and ensure Charles VII was crowned king at Reims.

Despite her initial fear, Joan came to have an unwavering belief in the divine nature of her visions. She claimed to have clasped the saints in embraces and insisted that the apparitions were real, not mere hallucinations. Joan's profound faith in her visions would ultimately drive her to take up arms and lead the French forces, playing a pivotal role in the Hundred Years' War.

Psychological Nature of Her Visions

As we look back to history and have a better understanding of human psychology, especially during times of war, some suggest alternative interpretations to Joan's recollections of her early visions. Some have suggested that she might have been schizophrenic or had epilepsy. The episodes that she experienced as divine visions could be consistent with a seizure disorder. According to Barbara Schildkrout in the *American Journal of Psychiatry*, "Given the episodic nature of Joan's symptoms, the clarity of her consciousness and thought between episodes, and the reasonableness of her self-defense, the comfort Joan took from the voices and visions suggests ecstatic auras. Evidence that her hallucinations were triggered by church bells aligns with reflex epilepsy....Recent reanalysis of Joan of Arc's testimony concluded that she likely had autosomal dominant lateral temporal epilepsy or idiopathic partial epilepsy with auditory features."[i]

In addition, Joan would have experienced the horrors of war early on in her young life, having grown up in a contested part of France. In 1425—right around the time she began to experience her visions—Domrémy was burned to the ground by the English army. Some historians look back to this context and reinterpret her visions not as divine visitations but as the result of psychological trauma or a symptom of PTSD.

Putting prophecies aside, Joan had a very practical motivation to end the war. As a caring and pious person, she would have wanted to end the suffering of her family and those in her village. Having grown up in an area independently loyal to the French Crown, she would have wanted to drive the enemy English out of her country.

These medical diagnoses can never be conclusive because they would require interviewing Joan of Arc or analyzing her brain using modern

---

[i] Barbara Schildkrout, "Joan of Arc-Hearing Voices," *American Journal of Psychiatry* 174, no. 12 (December 2017): 1153-1154, Https://psychiatryonline.org/doi/full/10.1176/appi.ajp.2017.17080948.

equipment. The only testimony we have is that of her trial, in which she defended her connection to the saints and stuck by her convictions. Whether or not her visions were "real," Joan managed to accomplish a seemingly impossible feat and continued to inspire French resistance for hundreds of years after she died.

"France Would Be Ruined by a Woman and Saved by a Virgin"

The claim that a young teenage girl had a vision from God likely would not have had much traction during the mid-fifteenth century had it not been for a few widely accepted prophecies that shaped the narrative around her. At that time, there was a prevailing belief that France would be "ruined by a woman and saved by a virgin." This prophecy was repeated as if it were a folk tale during the medieval period, greatly influencing popular opinion and giving Joan an open door to follow her visions out of Domrémy.

The prophecy gained particular prominence during the Hundred Years' War, which had started with Edward III's claim to the French throne via his maternal grandfather. And, only a few years before Joan's rise, Catherine of Valois—the daughter of Charles VI—died, clearing the way for Henry VI to make a renewed claim on the throne. France had been left in ruins after the disastrous deaths of two women. She was waiting for a virgin to save her.

Mythical Prophecies and "the Virgin"

The first prophecy, the one that had circulated in the stories of the French for years, came from the mythical figure of Merlin. The prophecies associated with Merlin were often cryptic and open to interpretation, but this one stated that the maid would come from the "Bois-Chenu"—the Oak Wood—typical of the landscape that surrounded Domrémy. The prophecy came to be seen as a divine endorsement of La Pucelle. The belief in Merlin's prophecies was so strong that both the French and the English saw them as credible predictions of future events. During the siege of Orléans in 1429, churchmen circulated lines attributed to Merlin, which were believed to foretell the coming of The Maiden. These lines were often in the form of chronograms, short inscriptions where the numerical values of the letters add up to significant dates—such as 1429, the year Joan began her military campaign.

Marie Robine of Avignon

Marie Robine of Avignon, also known as "La Gasque d'Avignon," was a French mystic who also had a prophecy of a virgin saving France. Marie's prophecies were less well-documented than Merlin's because she did not become a legendary figure in the same way, but they were nonetheless influential in her time. In the late fifteenth century, she reportedly came to the ailing King Charles VI and declared a vision for the future of a war-torn France. At Joan's nullification trial, Maître Jean Barbin testified to the prophecy and its influence on Charles VII at Chinon:

> "In the course of these deliberations Maitre Jean Erault stated that he had heard it said by Marie d'Avignon, (A woman called "la gasque d'Avignon," whose predictions made much stir at the beginning of the fifteenth century) who had formerly come to the King, that she had told him that the kingdom of France had much to suffer and many calamities to bear: saying moreover that she had had many visions touching the desolation of the kingdom of France, and amongst others that she had seen much armor which had been presented to her; and that she was alarmed, greatly fearing that she should be forced to take it; but it had been said to her that she need fear nothing, that this armor was not for her, but that a maiden who should come afterwards would bear these arms and deliver the kingdom of France from the enemy. And he believed firmly that Jeanne was the maiden of whom Marie d'Avignon thus spoke."[i]

Later, as Joan's successes and lore spread through the small nation, people began to connect her miracles to the prophecies of La Gasque d'Avignon and were further convinced that she was a divine miracle sent to save the French people.

---

[i] Virginia Frohlick, "Arrival at Chinon and the Trial at Poitiers" from *Saint Joan of Arc's Trial of Nullification*, The Saint Joan of Arc Center, accessed July 3, 2024, http://www.stjoan-center.com/Trials/null05.html.

Influence of the Prophecies

The prophecies of Merlin and Marie Robins created fertile ground for the acceptance of Joan of Arc and her claims. They allowed people to keep an open mind where they once may have dismissed the claims of a rural teenage girl. As Joan progressed on her campaign through France, more people saw her as the fulfillment of these prophecies, adding to the boost of morale the French military so desperately needed. The prophecies resonated deeply, especially in those areas that were loyal to France but occupied by the English—such as the Lorraine region, where Joan of Arc was born. Her humble origins, religious piety, saintly visions, and success in lifting the Siege of Orléans and securing the coronation of Charles VII all perfectly fulfilled the predictions made in the legends of Merlin and Marie Robins, helping to legitimize Joan's actions. The prophecies also invited closer scrutiny by the English, who searched for ways they could counter Joan's claims. Ultimately, the claims contributed to her legacy as a divinely inspired savior of France.

Leaving Domrémy

At the age of sixteen, Joan received the message that would cause her to leave her home and seek an audience with Charles VII. One of the voices, which she attributed to Saint Michael, was telling her that she must leave Domrémy to guide France to victory, beginning at Vaucouleurs. She resisted the voices for a long time, according to her testimony at trial, but finally, she set out on the path of her destiny in 1428 when she was only seventeen years old.

Chapter 2 – A Call to Arms

The French were facing the English army on the other side of the Loire. The English had just laid siege to Orléans and were threatening to do the same for the other fortifications along the Loire. The Dauphin seemed to be facing his final days, and his savior arrived in the form of the seventeen-year-old Jeanne d'Arc, or La Pucelle as she had come to be known. She arrived at the court on February 23, facing a skeptical audience of the Dauphin and his supporters. Before she could demand an army to help her lift the siege at Orléans, she had to prove her divine guidance.

But before that, she would have to persuade the captain at Vaucouleurs that she had the guidance that would save France.

Domrémy to Vaucouleurs

In 1428, Joan's visions and visitations finally reached a boiling point. She was compelled to meet the Dauphin and fulfill her fate of putting him on the throne. And so, she conspired to go to Vaucouleurs with an uncle, Durand Laxart. At her nullification trial, Laxart would claim she persuaded him, using the same prophecy we discussed in the previous chapter: "I went to fetch her from her father's and brought her to my house; she told me she wished to go into France, to the Dauphin, to have him crowned. 'Was it not foretold formerly,' she said to me, 'that France should be desolated by a woman, and should be restored by a maid?'"[i]

---

[i] Ben D. Kennedy, "Trial of Nullification (Rehabilitation) Vacouleurs and the Journey to

Laxart dutifully brought her to Vaucouleurs to visit the military captain stationed there, Robert de Baudricourt. Multiple times, Baudricourt told Joan's uncle to return her to her father so he could box her ears and refused to provide the armed escort Joan requested to reach the Dauphin's court at Chinon. But Joan kept returning, and as she did so her own notoriety grew throughout Vaucouleurs. Baudricourt was unmoved until, finally, Joan made a claim he could not ignore.

The Battle of the Herrings

Many miles away, just north of Orléans by the town of Rouvray, the Dauphin's forces met with the English in a short yet devastating battle. On February 12, 1429, many months into the Siege of Orléans, a small contingent of French soldiers attempted to intercept an English supply convoy. The French forces and their Scottish allies consisted of about four thousand men, which they thought would lead to an easy victory against the small English convoy. The English had about three hundred wagons carrying weapons, ammunition, and barrels of herrings to sustain their troops during the upcoming season of Lent—lending the battle its name. Unfortunately for the French, the English formed a solid defense, and the Scottish forces attacked prematurely, leading to a quick English victory. About six hundred men were lost on the French side.

Rouvray is about 200 kilometers (124 miles) away from Vaucouleurs, yet on that very same day, Joan came to Baudricourt and delivered the news that the Dauphin's army had suffered a great loss near Orléans. Baudricourt dismissed her again, but a few days later, a messenger arrived describing the crushing defeat of the Battle of the Herrings at Rouvray. This was the incontrovertible proof that Baudricourt needed to believe in what Joan of Arc was saying. There was no way she could have known, on the same day of the battle, that the French would suffer such a loss. The Battle of the Herrings was an opportunistic one, not a planned conflict in the war, and it occurred many miles south of Vaucouleurs. Joan could not have traveled that quickly through enemy territory and back again.

Baudricourt finally relented and granted Joan a small company of soldiers and armor to disguise herself along the journey. On February

Chinon," accessed July 5, 2024, www.maidofheaven.com/joanofarc_nullification_vaucouleurs_chinon.asp,

22, 1429, Joan and her escort departed Vaucouleurs to make the treacherous journey through enemy territory to the Dauphin's court at Chinon.

Chinon and Charles VII

The journey to Chinon was fraught with danger. Traveling over 600 kilometers (372 miles), Joan faced English and Burgundian patrols and roads teeming with thieves ready to take her party for all they were worth. Joan and her companions stopped only to observe mass and managed to make it to Chinon on March 5, 1429, eleven days after departing from Vaucouleurs. They first arrived at Sainte-Catherine-de-Fierbois before sending word that Joan wished to make an appearance to the Dauphin, supported by Captain Baudricourt. Before she could do so, Joan was examined by Yolande of Aragon.

Yolande of Aragon

Yolande of Aragon, Countess of Provence and Duchess of Anjou, was the Dauphin's stepmother and mother-in-law and had already become a huge influence in the Hundred Years' War. She persuaded the Duke of Brittany to end his alliance with the English, greatly diluting their forces in the north, and negotiated an alliance with Scotland, adding their forces to the French effort. She was also instrumental in setting up the Dauphin in southern France, protecting him from potential assassination had he remained in Paris.

Yolande was the one who heard Joan's story and saw the potential in this enthusiastic young maid. She arranged to have Joan's virginity verified at the Court of Anjou before arranging for her to be presented at the Dauphin's court. (Yolande of Aragon is another fascinating yet little-known female figure of the Hundred Years' War. We encourage anyone reading this book to dive into her biography as well!)

Yolande of Aragon and her two children praying before the Virgin Mary and the Child.^a

The Fateful Meeting

A few days after she arrived at Chinon, Joan was finally granted an audience with the Dauphin. Details of this meeting have become legend, as the Dauphin initially hid his identity from Joan. The Dauphin was reportedly still unconvinced of Joan's divine nature and wary of a stranger interrupting his court. He concealed his identity and hid himself within the crowd of courtiers, but this did not deter Joan. She strode up to the disguised Dauphin and was reported to have said: "Very illustrious Lord Dauphin, I am come, being sent on the part of God, to give succor to the kingdom and to you."[i] Their meeting was followed by a private conversation, one that has been lost to time as Joan never revealed what

---

[i] Ben D. Kennedy, "Joan of Arc & Charles VII: First Meeting," Maid of Heaven, accessed July 5, 2024, http://www.maidofheaven.com/joanofarc_charlesvii_firstmeet.asp.

she said to the Dauphin, even under interrogation. She gave him a sign from God that she was the one who would save France should she be given an army to do so. After this meeting, Charles sent her to Poitiers to be examined again by the Catholic clergy and theologians there. Her claims may have persuaded him, but Charles VII needed them to be verified by the Church before he could support her with an army.

Jeanne d'Arc, devant Charles VII, répond aux prélats qui l'interrogent by Gillot Saint-Evre. This painting shows the meeting of Joan of Arc and Charles VII.'

Examination at Poitiers

For over three weeks, Joan of Arc was questioned by a committee of bishops and theologians at Poitiers, the only formal center of theology that was still loyal to the Armagnac faction. The committee questioned her extensively about her visions, faith, and claims of divine guidance, mirroring another interrogation that would happen a few years later. During the interrogation, Joan demonstrated complete confidence and conviction in her divine mission, and ultimately the committee found nothing heretical in her claims. Even though the committee was skeptical of the teenage girl's mission, they decided she could be safely employed by the army and was not a spy for the English.

The examination at Poitiers was initially recorded in the "Book of Poitiers," a testimony of her interview. The "book" was referred to frequently during her trial at Rouen. However, the actual book has been lost to history. We only have a few sentences that survived via testimony at Joan's posthumous nullification trial.

Thanks to the influence of Yolande of Aragon, Joan was given a suit of armor, her own page, a banner, and a small contingent to begin the trek up to Orléans.

The Legendary Sword of Joan of Arc

Before this, while waiting for Charles VII's answer at Sainte-Catherine-de Fierbois, Joan's voices instructed her to find her own sword. They told her she would find it buried behind the altar at the church devoted to Saint Catherine. This gave the sword special significance to her since Saint Catherine was one of the angels who guided her missions. Finding a sword buried beneath an altar was not unusual. It was a typical practice for soldiers to offer their swords or armor as a gesture of thanks and devotion after a battle. In fact, later in her career, Joan would offer her plates of armor at the abbey church of Saint-Denis after a failed assault on Paris.

A miniature of Joan of Arc in her armor.[5]

The sword Joan found at Sainte-Catherine-de-Fierbois was described as having five crosses on it and being rusty when she found it, though the rust came away easily. The legend behind the sword is a story in and of itself. It was possibly the sword used by Charles Martel as he drove away the Muslim invasions of Aquitaine, left at the church after the Battle of Tours. This legend did not surface until after Joan's death, so it may have become popularized to connect the memory of Joan of Arc to another legendary savior of France. According to testimony at her trial, she never used this sword to kill anyone. It was mostly used to chase away prostitutes and camp followers, but it was made no less dear to The Maiden.

Departure from Chinon, an Army at Blois

Joan was given titular command of her company, an honor often bestowed upon religious figures who accompanied strategists into battle. This reflected her position as a woman and an adolescent as she rode into battle. This title did not stop Joan from making alliances with the commanders she was following to Orléans, as we will soon see. In late April, on their way to Orléans, her army stopped at Blois to join another contingent on their way north.

The earliest known drawing of Joan of Arc.[6]

Here, her famous banner, which would become a gleaming symbol The Maid carried into all her battles, was sewn. The banner was white with scattered fleurs-de-lys embroidered as a background. There was an image of God seated on a field, holding up the world, with his angels alongside him. The banner was fringed with gold silk, and on it was embroidered the words "Jhesus Maria."[i] Joan's company, along with the convoy of food for those trapped inside Orléans and an additional troupe of soldiers, departed for Orléans on April 29, 1429, where Joan's legacy would be cemented in a stunning display of enthusiasm, courage, and strategic brilliance. The French would see what she was capable of—and so would the English.

---

[i] "Portraits of a Saint: Her Journey," Saint Joan of Arc.com, accessed July 5, 2024, https://saint-joan-of-arc.com/journey.htm.

Chapter 3 – The Maiden at Orléans

The view of Orléans in the early 1400s.[7]

Initially meant to be a figurehead to help boost morale, Joan soon became a crucial element in the battles around the city, fighting alongside the other soldiers and pushing for aggressive assault tactics against the English. Joan's presence, to the French, signified a divine support that would help them in lifting the siege.

Siege of Orléans and the Hundred Years' War

The Siege of Orléans was a pivotal moment in the Hundred Years' War and a decisive turning point for French forces battling against the English. But why was this city so important? Part of the reason lies in the strategic importance of Orléans and the time the siege took place within the greater context of the war.

The siege took place over seven months, beginning in 1428. By this time, the Hundred Years' War had raged on for ninety-one years. About three or four generations had lived and died while the battle for the

French Crown occurred. To provide a modern example, if the Hundred Years' War had taken place in our time, the beginning of the war would have been in 1933—the height of the Great Depression and the rise of Hitler and the Nazi Party—and the Siege of Orléans would have taken place between 2023-2024. Consider how much has changed in our world within that time frame, and you can see why Joan's ascendance became so important to the French forces fighting against the English invasion at that time.

By 1428, the English wanted to strengthen their hold on France by pushing south of the Loire into solid Armagnac territory. Orléans was a strategic location on the Loire as the last major city between English-controlled northern France and the territories still loyal to Charles VII in the south. If the English could take control of Orléans, it would open the gates for the English to dominate central France and give them the power to take over the rest of the territory. On the other hand, if the French resisted and fought back against the English, it would reinvigorate their forces and provide a strategic post from which to push back and retake the northern part of the country. In this context, we see that the Siege of Orléans was not just a battle for a city but a tipping point for the course of the Hundred Years' War.

Timeline of the Siege of Orléans

The Siege of Orléans began on October 12, 1428, and ended on May 8, 1429. Joan of Arc's involvement lasted only nine days, beginning on April 29, 1429, but her impact on the morale of the French citizens and the battle strategies in the final days was decisive in lifting the siege. The following is a timeline of the events of the Siege of Orléans.

- <u>October 12, 1428</u>: The siege of Orléans formally begins under the command of Thomas de Montacute, Earl of Salisbury. After isolating Orléans, Salisbury consolidates his forces at Les Tourelles.
- <u>October 17, 1428</u>: English artillery bombardment of Orléans commences.
- <u>October 23, 1428</u>: French troops are driven into the fortified city of Orléans by the English artillery. They damage the nineteen-arch-bridge in their retreat.
- <u>November 3, 1428</u>: The Earl of Salisbury is fatally wounded by cannon fire while surveying the French military positions.

Command passes to William de la Pole, Earl of Suffolk, who is significantly less aggressive than Salisbury. Suffolk decides to pull away from the city, leaving behind William Glasdale and a small force of English soldiers to guard Les Tourelles.

- <u>December 1428</u>: John Talbot, Earl of Shrewsbury, and Thomas Scales arrive to reinforce the English siege, stimulating more aggressive operations. Shrewsbury moves his troops back to the city. He also builds additional forts along the Île de Charlemagne and at Saint-Loup and Saint-Jean-le-Blanc.

- <u>February 12, 1429</u>: The Battle of the Herrings. French troops and Scottish allies (led by Sir John Stewart of Darnley) attack a convoy of food headed toward Orléans that was intended for the English troops. French troops are brutally defeated by the English, causing them to flee. Joan, two hundred miles away at Vaucouleurs, tells Robert de Baudricort that "the Dauphin's arms that day suffered a great reverse near Orléans." When Baudricourt hears word of the Battle of the Herrings, he is forced to take Joan's word and arranges for her to meet with the Dauphin.

An illustration of the Battle of the Herrings.[8]

- <u>February 1429</u>: The city of Orléans applies for the protection of the Duke of Burgundy. The Duke of Bedford, ruling under Henry VI's name at Normandy, refuses the agreement, angering the Burgundians. Fifteen hundred Burgundian troops are withdrawn from Orléans, weakening the English army and supply lines.

- March 22, 1429: Joan of Arc sends a message to the King of England, his commanders, and the soldiers of his army: "I will make them flee the country, whether they wish to or not; and if they will not obey, The Maid will have them all killed. She comes sent by the King of Heaven, body for body, to take you out of France, and The Maid promises and certifies to you that if you do not leave France she and her troops will raise a mighty outcry as has not been heard in France in a thousand years."[i]
- April 29, 1429: Joan of Arc arrives at Blois with a relief force led by Jean de Dunois, bringing supplies and boosting morale. While not given formal command, she becomes a de facto leader due to her influence on troop morale and strategy. A strong wind reverses itself over the river, allowing French troops to sail into Orléans under the cover of darkness.
- April 30, 1429: Joan enters Orléans with supplies, inspiring the defenders.
- May 1, 1429: Joan assesses the English fortifications while Dunois returns to Blois for reinforcements. She exchanges words with William Glasdale and sends messages to the English troops, who accuse her of being a witch.
- May 4-8, 1429: Joan leads or inspires several successful assaults on English fortifications, including the capture of the fortresses of Saint-Loup, Saint-Jean-le-Blac, and Les Augustins. At Joan's request, the lives of the captured soldiers are spared.
- May 7, 1429: Joan is wounded during the assault on Les Tourelles but insists on returning for the second day of the assault, inspiring the people of Orléans.
- May 8, 1429: Les Tourelles is captured. The English lift the siege and retreat from Orléans.

Joan at Orléans

Even with the Dauphin's blessing, Joan faced skepticism from the military leaders, who initially saw her as a symbolic figurehead meant to

---

[i] Paul Halsall, "Medieval Sourcebook: Joan of Arc: Letter to the King of England, 1429," in *Internet Medieval Sourcebook*, Paul Halsall/Fordham University, November 1996, https://sourcebooks.fordham.edu/source/joanofarc.asp.

boost morale rather than a military strategist or a soldier on the front lines.

This skepticism was not without reason. Joan proved to be an aggressive strategist who preferred to face the English head-on at every chance. When she presented this idea to marshals Jean de La Brosse (Lord of Boussac) and Gilles de Rais, the commanders of her convoy, they deceived her and secretly led the procession around Orléans to approach from the south, which was safer. She was apparently indignant at the deception and angry that the commanders did not want to meet the English immediately.

It took the commander at Orléans, Jean de Dunois, to persuade Joan that it was necessary to wait for supplies and reinforcements from Blois before a formal confrontation could occur. Her response to the deception was to tell Dunois again of her heavenly mission—to deliver "succor" from the Kingdom of Heaven. With that, the winds over the Loire suddenly changed and allowed the troops to sail quietly into the city—an event that would later be described as one of her first saintly miracles.

Joan the Divine

According to documents from her nullification trial, Jean de Dunois said the following about Joan:

> "There was never anyone more sober. I often heard it said by the Sieur Jean d'Aulon, Knight, now Seneschal of Beaucaire, who had been appointed by the King to watch over her, as being the wisest and most worthy in the army, that he did not think there had ever been a more chaste woman. Neither I nor others, when we were with her, had ever an evil thought: there was in her something divine."[i]

This sentiment is echoed by other men in the army, all of whom suggest that Joan inspired the sort of awe that made the soldiers obey her in a way they would not have for another woman. It very well could have been a connection to God, or perhaps it was the impressive confidence of the teenage girl. Joan was, to the very end, steadfast in her convictions,

---

[i] Søren Bie, "Jean D'Arc's Trial of Nullification 1455," In *Jean d'Arc Maid of Orleans Deliverer of France*, edited by Douglass Murray (1902), Jeanne d'Arc la pucelle, accessed June 24, 2024, https://www.jeanne-darc.info/trial-of-nullification/.

and that determination was palpable to those around her. Her cause was aided by the vague prophecies that a "Maid from Lorraine" would be the savior of France—now here she was.

Joan the Soldier

During her procession from Chinon to Orléans, she forbade the typical rowdy or drunken behavior that would have been common for men of that time, even forcing them to marry any woman who was a camp follower or prostitute should the men succumb to temptation.

Joan of Arc enters Orléans by Jean-Jacques Scherrer.[9]

It was seen as almost miraculous that a woman—a girl of only seventeen at the time—could have such a hold on men much older than her. Dunois also testified that she joked with the men about war and yet held fast to her mission—to lift the siege at Orléans and lead Charles VII to be crowned at Reims.

Joan did not keep to a figurehead position, analyzing the position of the opposing army and even taunting them with the promise of salvation. She was invited by Dunois to a war council and insisted that Dunois needed to bring in more troops to launch an offensive against the English.

Arguably, her most aggressive move was the conversation she had with the leader of the English troops, William Glasdale, while Dunois was away. Joan had repeatedly sent messages and envoys to the English troops, prevailing upon them to give up and give in to God's command that Orléans should be controlled by the French. When they did not answer, Joan went out to meet them directly. Later, during her trial nullification, her page, Louis de Conte, said that Glasdale insulted Joan, calling her a cowgirl and threatening to burn her alive if she was captured by his troops. This did not deter Joan. She continued to study the English army's position and discuss military strategy with Dunois in preparation for meeting the English in battle and fulfilling her goal of taking back the city of Orléans.

Beginning of the End

On the first of May, Dunois left Orléans for Blois to gather reinforcements for the upcoming assault on the English fortresses around Orléans, meeting with two more French convoys as he came back to the city. French numbers were growing, and the English could do nothing but face them.

On the morning of May 4, 1429, the first of the final few battles for Orléans began—with Joan almost missing the fray as she lay down for a nap. She allegedly jumped out of bed, crying out: "Ha! Bloody boy, you did not tell me the blood of France was being shed!"

She could not have known the extent of the battle, which was initially meant to be a diversion tactic. Talbot attempted to draw some of the 1,500 French soldiers north of the city but was met by a small sortie. Seeing that his troops were outnumbered (1,500 to 400), Talbot retreated, leading the English back to their forts away from the waves of French troops. The quick victory boosted French morale and marked the beginning of a series of assaults that brought Orléans back into French hands.

The French battalion paused their strike for a day to rest and observe a feast day before resuming their assault on the English fortresses surrounding the city—but this time, they were not alone. As they were preparing to attack Les Augustins, they were joined by groups of citizen militia who were inspired by Joan's performance in battle and conviction in God. Joan launched a preemptive attack on the Boulevart only to draw English troops out of the fortress, forcing the French to fall back. According to legend, Joan raised her hand and shouted, "In the name of God!" That was enough to halt the advancing British troops and rally the French once again. Joan redirected the assault to Les Augustins, which was less guarded by the English, and by the end of the day, the French had taken another fortress from the English.

Les Tourelles: The Final Battle

By May 7, the English troops were battered, wounded, and sequestered in the last fortified garrison they held at Orléans. Les Tourelles was the most important stronghold as it was the bridgehead leading into the city. Whoever controlled the tower would control the main throughway for troops and supplies coming in and out of Orléans.

On the morning of May 7, the French, led by Joan of Arc, attacked the tower via the south bank of the Loire. Meanwhile, the citizen militia began repairing the bridge so they could aid in the attack from within the city. The assault began in the morning and included bombarding the highly fortified tower and ramming burning barges into the drawbridge to undermine the tower's foundation.

The attempt to blow the English out of Les Tourelles seemed fruitless. By the end of the day, Dunois was considering calling off the attack and starting again in the morning, but Joan convinced him to press on. She led the way herself and was swiftly struck down by a crossbow arrow in the shoulder.

Joan of Arc during the siege of Orléans by Eugène Lenepveu.[10]

Joan was quickly taken away as the English jeered that they had killed the witch who led the French troops. Later, at her nullification trial, Dunois testified that the arrow pierced Joan between the neck and shoulder, embedding itself about half a foot deep into her flesh. Joan rode her horse away from the action to pray in peace. After a short time,

Joan returned, apparently having pulled the arrow out herself, and rushed the tower again. With renewed confidence, the French soldiers followed her, managing to storm the tower and drive out the English. William Glasdale attempted to retreat across the burning drawbridge, but the bridge gave way, and he fell into the Loire and drowned under the weight of his armor. Without their leader, the English surrendered to the French. All in all, it was one of the bloodiest battles in the war, with approximately one thousand casualties on the English side.

Aftermath of the Siege

The drawbridge was swiftly repaired, and Joan symbolically rode across it to celebrate the victory at Orléans. When she entered Orléans, she paraded through the city on a white horse, repeating her familiar phrase: "The Lord has sent me to succor this good town of Orléans. Hope in God. If you have good hope and faith in him, you shall be delivered from your enemies."[i] She also boosted morale by giving the citizens of Orléans much-needed food and money.

While the battle was an important one for the French, it would not be the last. The towns surrounding Orléans were still under English control, and if Joan was going to succeed in her mission to lead Charles VII to his crown at Reims, the English would have to be defeated to secure safe passage for The Maid and the Dauphin.

Joan's reputation was solidified as a divine inspiration, miracle worker, and an incredible woman who would fight alongside the French forces. The English, meanwhile, realized that Joan's fame and the admiration she garnered from the French citizens would be dangerous to their cause and the military efforts in France—likely motivating them to think of how to nip Joan's influence in the bud.

---

[i] Don Hollway, "Joan of Arc and the Siege of Orléans," Warfare History Network, accessed June 24, 2024, https://warfarehistorynetwork.com/joan-of-arc-siege-of-orleans/.

Chapter 4 – The Triumph at Reims

After the victory at Orléans, Joan left Dunois behind, intent on making her way back to Chinon to lead the Dauphin Charles VII to his coronation. But, before that could happen, a few obstacles needed to be cleared from their path.

The Path to Coronation

It was essential for Joan to see Charles VII become king. Besides her holy mission, she likely knew it was the only way the French could decisively drive the English out once and for all. Generations of French kings had been crowned at Reims Cathedral, but the city and the surrounding area were occupied by the English. Charles VII, fearing for his safety, stayed south of the Loire and so could not secure his claim to the French throne. Acting on the momentum from the victory at Orléans, Joan led the French troops in their mission to clear a safe passage for Charles to finally legitimize his claim, boost French morale, and create a sense of nationalistic unity and pride for the country.

Clearing the Way: Battles of Jargeau, Meung-sur-Loire, and Beaugency

The battles of Jargeau, Meung-sur-Loire, and Beaugency were crucial to securing safe passage for the coronation procession to Reims. Without clearing these towns and defeating the fortresses along the Loire, the march to Reims would have been bloodier and may not have been successful.

The Battle of Jargeau happened over two days in June, a little over a month after the siege at Orléans was lifted. Jargeau was a small town on the Loire just east of Orléans and was strategically important thanks to its fortified bridge across the river. Jargeau was the first offense directed by Joan, who used tactics similar to what she used to lift the siege of Orléans. Using artillery to attack the foundation of the towers and destroy the ramparts weakened the English ground forces. As she had with Orléans, Joan charged with the front lines, and the men followed her banner into battle.

Meung-sur-Loire was the next target, on the opposite side of Orléans. On June 15, only three days after the Battle of Jargeau, French forces captured the town's bridge and cut off the path for any potential English reinforcements to make their way south of the Loire. The next day, the French attacked Beaugency on the northern bank of the Loire, decimating the English garrison in only two days.

Using the momentum of three back-to-back battles allowed the French to ride high on their victories and made it difficult for the weary English forces to rest or reinforce their armies. The English had been waiting for a force of five thousand to arrive from Paris since the siege of Orléans. The three losses demoralized the English, who finally felt the weight of the larger French army.

The Battle of Patay

The final battle in the short Loire Campaign occurred on June 18, 1429. Forces from Paris led by Sir John Falstaff and Sir John Talbot, Earl of Shrewsbury, had finally arrived to help defend the English position along the river—only to find out that the English had lost all three of their most strategic posts in an onslaught the week before. The English retreated, pausing at Patay to rest, with a small band of archers across the road to protect them from a French column. What they did not think to protect themselves from was wildlife.

The French, hoping to uncover the English position, flushed out a stag from the forest, sending it running through the English camp. The English sent up a hunting cry to get the deer and were suddenly ambushed by Étienne "La Hire" de Vignolles, Jean Poton de Xaintrailles, and 1,500 men. The English were swiftly defeated by La Hire, Xaintrailles, and the rest of the French line that swept through the

English flanks. The battle decimated the English longbow lines, which were a significant element in their military strategy. Until the Battle of Patay, the English fought using a line of longbowmen who stood behind a border of sharpened stakes. The stakes would cut down an approaching cavalry as the archers behind them unleashed their arrows. With the surprise attack at Patay, the English were unable to establish their lines in time and were overwhelmed by the onslaught of French forces.

The Bloodless March

With these three strategic garrisons defeated, the French cleared the way for their procession to Reims. Word of Joan's bravado and battle strategy had spread, and as the procession passed through Burgundian territory, towns opened their gates to Joan and her followers.

For those that did not, Joan used a combination of diplomacy and a show of force to persuade them. At Troyes, Joan sent letters to the city promising they would be pardoned if they surrendered peacefully. When they still did not open their gates, she organized a show of force, reminding the residents of the recent series of victories and her reputation as an aggressive and successful leader. After four days, they gave over the keys to the city, and the procession to Reims was allowed to continue.

The army finally reached Reims on July 16, 1429. The city opened its gates to the now-famous Joan of Arc, the Maid of Orléans who had liberated the Loire from the French. The stage was now set for Charles VII's coronation.

Coronation of the Dauphin, Charles VII

Reims Cathedral had been used as the site of French coronations since the ninth century when (according to French legend) a dove descended from the skies holding a vial of holy oil, which the bishop used to baptize the first King of the Franks.

The coronation ceremony took place on July 17, 1429, and was attended by the Archbishop of Reims, Renault Chartres; the Bishop of Laon, William of Champeaux; and the Bishop of Châlons, Jean Saarbrücken. The coronation of the king needed to be attended by a certain number of noblemen and religious figures (peers of the king). Since the coronation was during wartime in lands that were held by Burgundian forces, Charles raised members of his procession to nobility to satisfy that requirement. The ceremony was simple, without the traditional symbols of his office since the scepter and crown were still held in Paris—deep in English territory.

The ceremony lasted about five hours, beginning with the Dauphin's private prayers at 9:00 a.m. He was knighted by the Duke of Alençon, Joan's closest ally, and a crown was placed on his head by Archbishop Chartres. Throughout the ceremony, Joan stood by dressed in her armor, draped with a white silk tunic, her banner held high beside her. Her presence served as a reminder of what had led to this moment—a landslide of French victories and a newly unified and emboldened French military. Her divine mission was now fulfilled, and she believed she would be able to return home to Domrémy once the kingship was secured.

Joan of Arc at the coronation of Charles VII by Jean-Auguste-Dominique Ingres.[ii]

After the ceremony, Joan knelt before the newly anointed King Charles VII. She embraced his legs and said, "Noble King, now is accomplished the pleasure of God, who willed that I should raise the siege of Orléans, and should bring you to this city of Reims to receive your holy coronation, thus showing that you are the true King, him to whom the throne of France must belong."[i]

---

[i] Allen Williamson, "Joan of Arc Biography – Segment 8: The March to Rheims," Joan of Arc Archive, accessed June 27, 2024, https://joan-of-arc.org/joanofarc_life_summary_rheims.html.

Why Was The Coronation Crucial?

The English claimant to the French throne, Henry VI, had been crowned without the holy anointed oil and in Paris—and this was seen as an illegitimate coronation. By arriving at Reims, the traditional site of coronation in France, and being anointed with the holy oil, Charles made himself the true king in the eyes of the French people. At this point in the Hundred Years' War, that was extremely important. His coronation galvanized the French people's resistance against the English, persuaded some of the hesitant French to join his cause, and strengthened his case against the Duke of Burgundy's claim to the land. The symbolic power of a crowned and anointed King of France rallied support not only from the Armagnac-controlled areas of France but also from those in the north who had been living under English rule.

It was as much a political move as a symbolic one. With his coronation, Charles' armies fought under the French banner. Since Joan was such a popular figure, her claim that he was the one true king, according to her messages from God, transferred some of the popularity to him. With this unifying force, the French received the boost in morale that they needed to begin fighting aggressively in the war and turning the tides in their favor.

Commemorative plaque for Joan of Arc. It says, "Jeanne d'Arc made sacred Charles VII at Reims on July 17, 1429. She accomplished her mission." [12]

After the Coronation

Joan's legacy had been cemented when she stood as the only woman by Charles' side when he was anointed as king. This period represents the height of Joan of Arc's influence and her stunning achievements. In three short months, she had ended a seven-month-long siege at Orléans, led a stunning military campaign through the Loire Valley, and fulfilled her mission to crown the Dauphin as the next King of France. The prophecy of the maiden from Lorraine had come true, but soon the winds would change, and Joan would find herself in dangerous waters.

Chapter 5 – The Capture

Joan's successful campaigns and her ability to get Charles to his rightful coronation seat drew a large target on her back for the English and Burgundians. She excited the French into an offensive position in the Hundred Years' War when, for years, they had merely retreated and defended their territory. Joan's success was an obstacle to the advancement of the English claim, and the Burgundians were wary of the growing number of French citizens who were inspired by the young girl. The English already saw her as a heretic and possibly even a witch. A smear campaign was not out of the question if they could capture Joan and imprison her. Unfortunately for Joan, after Charles' coronation, he began to lean more on his advisors, who were also wary of Joan and the influence she seemed to have over the newly crowned king. This combination of forces whirled around Joan, creating the circumstances that led to her capture and, eventually, her execution.

Liberation of Northern France

The English had finally been driven out of the Loire Valley, and Joan was eager to continue her aggressive campaign to liberate Northern France, but the new king was wary of launching an assault on the English and their allies. He preferred to retreat down the Loire and allow his courtiers to negotiate peace with the Duke of Burgundy, Philip the Good. Their conflicting strategies would eventually be her downfall as Joan began to lose the support of the king.

Siege of Paris, September 1429

Following Charles VII's coronation, Joan immediately set her eyes on Paris, the capital city and an early stronghold for the English. The city of Paris hated Charles VII, nicknaming him "Petit Roi de Bourges" (Little King of Bourges) for the fact that he hid away in a little town rather than launch an offense for the capital city. Joan believed that capturing Paris would be a major step in re-unifying France under Charles VII's name and persuaded him to launch an attack on the city in September 1429.

Joan of Arc during the siege of Paris.[13]

After stopping at Saint-Denis, Joan launched the attack on the walls of Paris alongside the Duke of Alençon, now an inseparable military partner. As in the other sieges, the French artillery attacked the foundations of the fortified walls as their soldiers poured over the moat. However, the citizens of Paris, along with the English battalion, put up a strong defense. Even with Joan's rallying cry, the French were unable to breach the walls of the city. After four hours of battle, and with Joan wounded by a crossbow arrow, King Charles VII ordered a retreat and took his army back to Gien, about 150 kilometers south of Paris. Joan sacrificed her signature white armor at the Abbey of Saint-Denis and would not experience another victory in battle.

Why Was the Siege Less Successful?

Going into the Siege of Paris, there were many factors that would doom the French. For starters, the Parisians at this time preferred English rule to the perceived terror of the Armagnacs. The English had given the Parisian nobility rights and freedoms that had been stripped away from them by the previous French kings and launched a successful propaganda campaign against the Armagnac, presenting them as violent and crude leaders. Charles VII overestimated Joan's power of personality and seemed to think the doors of Paris would open for her the way so many towns had capitulated to The Maid on the road to the coronation. Instead, the Parisians, loyal to the English, defended their city against the girl and her armies. Finally, unlike the Siege of Orléans, the English were well-equipped and plenty in number, so this time they were a more equal match for the French in firepower.

Political Challenges after Paris

With the defeat at Paris, the French (in particular, Charles VII) went back to their old wartime strategy of retreat and defense. Charles led his company back to Bourges, where he felt safe, and began to develop a strategy of diplomacy with the Burgundians. At this point, it seemed obvious that if the French allied with the Burgundian forces, they could definitively drive out the English and have more manpower on the battlefield. Not only that, but Charles VII was starting to run out of money. Part of the reason he was unable to sustain a long-term siege at Paris was the trouble with paying his military. An alliance with the Burgundians would help to alleviate this stress. Charles spent the winter along the Loire, and as time passed, Joan's influence over him began to wane. It is possible he felt her popularity and influence were beginning to eclipse his own. Regardless, her army was disbanded, and she spent the winter as a courtier, frequently making trips to visit the poor. In the spring, the lands near Champagne and Reims were once again vulnerable and coming under attack from the Duke of Burgundy.

The Capture at Compiègne

On May 23, 1430, Joan led a sortie from Compiègne against the Burgundian forces who surrounded the town. They were initially successful, pushing the opposing troops back to Margny. However, the tide quickly turned as the Burgundian leader, John of Luxembourg, called for reinforcements. English and Burgundian reinforcements quickly arrived, outnumbering the French. French commanders ordered a retreat to Compiègne, but Joan refused and held back to help protect soldiers who were retreating to the city. In the confusion, the city gates were closed before they could all get back inside, leaving Joan stranded. Surrounded by enemy forces, Joan was pulled down from her horse by an archer from the Burgundian troops. After a year of fighting and inspiring her countrymen, Joan was captured and imprisoned by the enemy.

Part of the frieze depicting Joan's life in the Panthéon in Paris. This section illustrates Joan of Arc's capture at Compiègne.[14]

Joan, the Prisoner

Among the French, the news that Joan had been captured was a disaster. They mourned the woman they had come to see as a symbol of divine favor for their country and were demoralized by her imprisonment. In the loyalist towns of France, such as Compiègne, the news was met with fear for the future as the French worried that their new occupiers would retaliate against them for resisting alongside Joan. Meanwhile, advisors to the king tried to shift blame onto Joan by saying she was captured because she had ignored Charles VII's orders to leave Compiègne as he negotiated a truce with the Duke of Burgundy. In Paris, the bishops at the University of Paris demanded that Joan be turned over to them to face either the Grand Inquisitor or the Bishop of Beauvais, Pierre Cauchon, so she could answer to their charge of heresy.

As far as the historical record goes, Joan was treated fairly well by her Burgundian captors, most likely because she was a very valuable prisoner. John of Luxembourg knew the English would pay dearly for her, and it is possible he thought he would have the upper hand while negotiating with Charles VII if he had La Pucelle in his custody. Unfortunately for Joan, Charles VII did not seem to be interested in securing her freedom, possibly because he was trying to negotiate a truce with the Duke of Burgundy or was unhappy with Joan's popularity.

In the end, the English won out, and in November 1430, Joan was transferred to their custody for a ransom of ten thousand francs. By January 1431, Joan was imprisoned at Bouvreuil, awaiting her trial in Rouen, the capital of English-controlled Normandy.

Beginning of the End

Rouen would be the site of the final, tragic chapter of Joan of Arc's young life. La Pucelle, who had led armies and unified and inspired her nation, now found herself alone in a hostile prison facing an unsympathetic court determined to discredit her. Her English captors and their religious allies set the stage for a trial that would define Joan's legacy beyond her short life, mark Joan's transformation into a martyr, and can be seen as a pivotal moment in the Hundred Years' War.

Chapter 6 – Trial of Faith

As we mentioned, Joan of Arc's trial is one of the most thoroughly documented and well-preserved legal proceedings from the medieval period, offering historians a great amount of insight into how both secular and ecclesiastical trials might have been conducted at the time. Her trial was transcribed in Latin (the formal language of the Catholic Church) and French.

Irregularities at Trial

Even for the medieval period, Joan's trial and interrogations were highly irregular, demonstrating the political motivations behind the decision to put her on trial. The strangest of all of these irregularities was the fact that she was being tried at Rouen by a bishop from Reims. Rouen was firmly in the Normandy region of France, had been the capital city for the English since the start of the war, and was located three hundred kilometers away from Reims—the region in which Joan was captured. There were various reasons for this, the most significant being that Joan was captured by Burgundian forces and sold as a prisoner to the English.

Imprisonment and Interrogation

As a military prisoner in Rouen, she was pitted against men who were determined to manipulate her words and force her to reject her beliefs. In the introduction to the English translation of her trial, Coley Taylor details it as such:

"Most of her judges were graduates and members of the faculty of the University of Paris which at that time served the church through a kind of dictatorship of the General Council. Many of them had served the King of England or his regent the Duke of Bedford, as ambassadors or councillors. Nearly all of them were at one time or another on the English payroll, directly, or indirectly through ecclesiastical appointments that were in the hands of the English King. We see Jeanne pitted against sixty skilled politicians, lawyers, ambassadors, trained in all the complexities of legal questioning, all of them versed in academic casuistry. Most of them were avowedly her enemies. Her victories for Charles VII had driven many of them, including Bishop Cauchon, out of their dioceses, away from their seats of authority and revenue. They were of the University of Paris and Jeanne had threatened Paris. If she had succeeded in that they would have been utterly ruined. She was imprisoned, not in the ecclesiastical prison where women would have attended her, but in the Castle of Rouen, at that time the English citadel, governed by the Earl of Warwick. The little English king lived there, and the regent Bedford. Jeanne was closely guarded and was kept in irons even when she was extremely ill. Her guards annoyed her and abused her and she lived in constant fear of them, although Warwick restrained them somewhat, for she was a valuable prisoner; the English had paid 10,000 livres for her. Ten or twelve francs was the price of a horse."[i]

    Joan's trial was conducted a bit differently than trials today. Rather than presenting her case in court in front of a judge, with a jury of her peers to decide on her guilt, Joan was interrogated repeatedly over several months before her testimony was summarized and submitted for consideration by the clergy at the University of Paris. She was provided no legal counsel (to which she was entitled) and was forced to act as the sole witness both for and against herself. She was kept isolated, had no way to prepare her case, and was frequently intimidated by her

---

[i] Paul Halsall, "Medieval Sourcebook: The Trial of Joan of Arc," in *Internet Medieval Sourcebook*, Paul Halsall/Fordham University, September 1999, https://sourcebooks.fordham.edu/basis/joanofarc-trial.asp.

adjudicator, who was also her accuser. Joan was uneducated and still a minor, and comments made in her support were frequently struck from the record. Her interrogation shows that her trial was biased against her from the start. They used the threat of torture, as well as intrigue, to try to force her to betray herself:

> "But perhaps among so many instances of cruelty and bigotry, the most infamous act of all the many in this tragedy was that performed by the Canon Nicolas Loiseleur, a creature of Cauchon, as false, as cruel, and as unscrupulous as his master and patron. This reverend scoundrel had, at the beginning of the trial, by his feigned sympathy for the prisoner, wormed himself into Joan of Arc's confidence. He told her that he, too, came from near her home, that he in his heart of hearts belonged to the French side, that he was a prisoner on account of his known devotion to Charles and to France, and many other such lies. This Judas—half in the character of a layman, half in that of a confessor, and wholly as a sympathetic friend and a fellow-sufferer—paid the prisoner long visits, disguised both as priest and layman, as the part suited the day's action best. Loiseleur actually used the means of extracting information from Joan of Arc under the seal of confession, to be afterwards employed against her by Cauchon. While these conversations and confessions took place, Warwick and Cauchon would be concealed in a part of the dungeon from which they could overhear what passed between the two—one of whom worthily might be called an angel, the other truthfully a devil. With the Bishop and knight—whose conduct as regards Joan of Arc deeply tarnished an otherwise high character—were seated clerks, who wrote down what passed in these meetings. The clerks, to their credit, are said to have at first refused to comply with doing such dirty work."[i]

These tricks of intrigue and wording would continue, even after her sentence. The goal of Joan's trial was not to put her on the stand and answer the ecclesiastical doubts of those judging her. Instead, their goal was to undermine Joan's legacy to achieve a political goal. In many ways,

---

[i] Ben D. Kennedy, "Joan of Arc Chapter 5 Imprisonment and Trial," Maid of Heaven Foundation, accessed June 29, 2024,
http://www.maidofheaven.com/joanofarc_gower_imprisonment_trial.asp.

this can be seen as a propaganda trial rather than a criminal or religious one, since the English were using Joan's popularity to discredit her. Joan had provided morale and hope for the French soldiers, and the English hoped that by claiming she was a heretic they would lose their faith in their "savior." Joan had also given the French the belief that God ordained the lands in conflict to the French. By casting doubt on her word, they could also cast a shadow over this divine claim. Finally, if they were able to say she was guilty of heresy, the coronation of Charles would be seen as illegitimate since she was lying about her connection to God and the divine right to put Charles on the throne.

Ecclesiastical Politics

The power structures of Europe during the Hundred Years' War were a tight braid of secular and religious institutions. As mentioned in the quote from Joan's trial, the University of Paris was an arm of the Catholic Church at the time. Most of her judges were clergymen and theologians from the University of Paris who were educated in matters of the church—but also deeply involved in the politics of the Hundred Years' War. In 1431, the university was aligned with the English and Burgundian factions of the war, so they were politically biased against Joan of Arc and her assertions of divine guidance for France. So, while the arguments at trial may have been religious ones, the motivations behind them were secular as the university wanted to reinforce the English position in the war.

Some of the 120 clerics were reluctant participants in the trial (or so they claimed at her nullification), while others saw the trial as an opportunity to advance their ecclesiastical and political careers. Ultimately, the trial exposed the vulnerability of the Catholic Church to political manipulation and how desperate they were to maintain their authority.

Joan's claim that she received direct communications from God threatened the Catholic Church's hierarchy and claim that it had a monopoly on spiritual communication. The Church also clearly feared what might happen if the French successfully invaded Paris and possibly retaliated against the clergymen still installed there.

Pierre Cauchon, Bishop of Beauvais

Pierre Cauchon (1371-1442) was born near Reims (the site of Charles' coronation) and studied at the University of Paris, where he eventually became the rector in 1403. During his time at the University of Paris, he studied liberal arts, canon law, and theology.

It is important to understand that in this period, the Roman Catholic Church in Europe was not only a spiritual or religious institution but an important political entity. The pope and his bishops often acted as advisors to rulers across the continent, influencing many of their state decisions. The Church owned vast swathes of land on which it collected tithes, enabling it to wield much economic power, and it provided social services like education and healthcare through monasteries and convents. The influence of the Catholic Church was all-encompassing in medieval Europe, and a high position in the Church came with incredible power. Cauchon was likely educating himself with an eye for one of these more powerful positions, as evidenced by his involvement in Joan of Arc's trial.

Early in his career, Cauchon aligned himself with the Burgundian faction of the Hundred Years' War. In 1420, he became the Bishop of Beauvais in Northern France and began to serve as a counselor to the young Henry VI of England, as well as John, Duke of Bedford, the English king's emissary in France.

When Joan liberated Reims from the Burgundians, Cauchon was forced to leave his diocese and return to Paris, which may have influenced his desire to see her captured and tried. As the primary judge at her trial, Cauchon presided over the arguments against Joan as well as her interrogation. His actions were later seen as corrupt and guided by English interests, in addition to his ambition for advancement in the Church.

Pierre Cauchon presides over Joan of Arc's trial.[15]

In 1432, a year after Joan's execution, Cauchon was promoted to Bishop of Lisieux, where he spent the rest of his life, having never achieved his goal of becoming Archbishop of Rouen. He died on December 18, 1442. In 1456, after the Nullification Trial, the Catholic Church overturned his verdict, with many condemning his extension of secular politics into a supposedly religious trial.

Public and Private Interrogation

The interrogations began in January 1431 and continued until Joan's execution on May 30 of the same year. There were both public and private sessions in which Cauchon and the other clerics, nobility, and members of the University of Paris questioned Joan about her claims. She was questioned on a wide range of topics including her visions, military activities, relationship with the Catholic Church, her piety, and even the private conversations between herself and Charles VII.

The atmosphere at Rouen Castle was tense during the public interrogations. Joan was alone, facing the panel of her judges and accusers (who were one and the same). These sessions were not attended by the "public." Rather, they were called "public" in retrospect to differentiate them from the more intense sessions. They were intended to demonstrate that Joan's trial was being conducted fairly and openly, without the public's knowledge of the private interrogations that went on in her tower.

The private sessions that took place within her prison cell began about halfway through the trial, in March 1431. These sessions were attended by a much smaller group, led by Bishop Cauchon, with a notary to record what happened. They were more focused, and the interrogators questioned Joan without interruption, sometimes touching on more intrusive topics. They attempted to entrap her with complex questions about theology or trick her into making incriminating statements. Joan, however, maintained her composure and managed to answer them clearly every time. In one example, when asked by Cauchon if she was in God's grace, she famously answered, "If I am not, may God put me there; and if I am, may God so keep me."

The most dramatic of these private interrogations occurred on May 9, 1431, when Joan was threatened with physical torture unless she spoke the truth. The trial document describes the scene in detail:

> "To speak the truth to Us on divers and numerous points on which she had hitherto refused to reply or had replied untruthfully, the which are established in the highest degree by informations, proofs, and grave presumptions. A great number of these points was read and shown to her. Then she was told that, if she would not tell the truth, she would immediately be put to the torture, the instruments of which were here, in this same tower, under her eyes. There also were present the executioners, who by Our order had made all the necessary preparations for torturing her, in order to bring her back by this means into the way and knowledge of the truth, and thus to procure for her salvation both of body and soul, which she did expose to such grave peril by her lying inventions. To which Jeanne replied in this manner: 'Truly if you were to tear me limb from limb, and separate soul from body, I will tell you

nothing more; and, if I were to say anything else, I should always afterwards declare that you made me say it by force.'"[i]

The power and piety of the teenager was underestimated by the clerics interrogating her. Seeing how steadfast she was, and probably realizing they had more to lose if she appeared to have been physically tortured, the judges in attendance decided against torturing Joan. The interrogations were designed to break Joan's spirit and lure her into a confession, but she consistently maintained her story throughout the entire trial. Instead, the trial documents had the opposite effect, showing that Joan kept her faith and courage even while facing the threat of execution. Without realizing it, the English cemented Joan's legacy in history and made her a martyr. She might have faded into obscurity had they allowed her to continue fighting and losing on the battlefield.

Charges Against Joan

There were, at first, seventy articles of accusation against Joan, which were later reduced to twelve by Maître Nicolas Midi. The twelve articles directly address Joan's various claims that she had been sent on a mission by God and had been visited by Saint Catherine, Michael, and Margaret; that she wore men's dress; that she was tyrannous and cruel; that she disobeyed God's commandment by leaving her mother and father; that she was suicidal, a liar, and a blaspheme; that she was idolatrous and invoked demons; and finally, that she was a schismatic (someone who intentionally causes a division, in this case a division in the unity of the Church). The full list, including the descriptions of the articles and how her judges came to their conclusions, is now available online from various sources, having been archived and translated into many languages. Links to some of these can be found at the end of this book.

At the presentation of these articles, Joan continued to maintain everything she said, even if she would be thrown into a pyre and burned for her crimes.

---

[i] Douglas O. Linder, "Deliberations, Final Trial Session, and Sentence (May 9-23, 1431)," UMKC School of Law: Famous Trials, accessed June 30, 2024, https://www.famous-trials.com/the-trial-of-joan-of-arc-1431/2371-deliberations-final-trial-session-and-sentence-may-9-23-1431.

Chapter 7 – Martyrdom and Aftermath

The execution of Joan of Arc, on May 30, 1431, marked a significant turning point in the Hundred Years' War. Joan's martyrdom did not drastically alter the war. However, it had profound political and nationalistic repercussions that influenced its course and led to the rehabilitation of her legacy after the devastating heresy trial at Rouen.

Conditions in the Jail at Rouen

To extract Joan's cooperation, Cauchon and his inquisitors used brutal tactics to "break" Joan. First, they placed her in a military prison rather than an ecclesiastical one. This meant Joan was unable to attend mass and was guarded by English soldiers rather than Catholic nuns, a deep violation for the pious Joan. Second, they placed her in the Donjon of Rouen, a heavily guarded tower in the military fortress considered escape-proof. During her stay, she was kept chained to a wooden beam in her cell and kept in an iron cage for over fifty days. All this was to make it impossible for Joan to escape and rejoin the French forces—and to humiliate her as much as possible.

The Donjon of Rouen still stands today, an imposing figure over the small city, and can be visited by the public. The tower runs consistent tours that talk about Joan's imprisonment and execution and has a small museum dedicated to her memory.

Was Joan Raped or Assaulted?

One question that has plagued historians is whether Joan was raped or sexually assaulted during her time at Rouen. It was unlikely, as the guards watching over her were dutiful to a fault and would not have risked assaulting such an important prisoner. But the threat of rape or assault was always there. Since Joan was being watched day and night by English guards and chained to a wooden beam, she would have no way of protecting herself should one of the guards decide to turn against his duties of protection.

It is also likely that the threat of rape or assault motivated Joan to wear men's clothing for protection. A woman's dress would not provide any sort of barrier, while a man's tunic and breeches could. So, while it was unlikely that Joan of Arc was raped during her imprisonment, the threat of rape or sexual assault was used against her to force her submission and execution.

Abjuration, Recantation, Execution

Had the English allowed Joan of Arc to live, they would be running the risk that Charles VII would come to rescue her. During the time of her trial and imprisonment, Charles VII was deep in negotiations with the Burgundians and could not risk launching a mission to rescue Joan of Arc—but that situation could change. Cauchon had already succeeded at discrediting Joan with a trial based on manipulated testimonies and confessions, but he had yet to deliver that final blow.

Abjuration

On May 24, 1431, after months of interrogation, imprisonment, and a corrupt trial, Joan was brought to the Abbatiale Saint-Ouen cemetery for a public ceremony in which she was expected to renounce her claims of divine guidance and admit to the charges of heresy. Cauchon then presented Joan with two choices: sign an abjuration document or face immediate execution. According to the terms of the abjuration, Joan was required to renounce her visions, admit that she had been lying about her divine connection to God, and swear she would not wear men's clothing. In doing so, her sentence would be changed from execution to life imprisonment, in which Joan would also submit to the authority of the Church.

At first, Joan refused. She maintained that she had been visited by the saints Michael, Catherine, and Margaret and that she had been following God's will when she led the French army. In response to her hesitation,

Cauchon intimidated her by showing her the executioner and his cart, ready to take her to be burned that very day. Fearing for her life, Joan was coerced into signing the abjuration. But, being illiterate, she was unable to read the document. Historians debate whether the statements were read to her and she was then presented with a longer document to sign, or if Cauchon took advantage of her primitive signature (the simple icon of a cross) and later changed the paper that Joan signed for a much more complicated document. Either way, Joan would not have known the full extent of what she agreed to.

Recantation

It did not take long for Joan to recant, though it is difficult to say whether she wanted to do so. A condition of her signature was that Joan would be allowed to have a female companion and be allowed to attend mass—but those promises never materialized. Instead, she was returned to her tower, chained again to a wooden beam, and watched over by the same frightening English soldiers—with no one to protect her modesty now that she was forced to wear a dress.

The event that elicited her recantation was yet another manipulation. She argued with her captors, who refused to allow Joan to attend mass. As a result, her dress was taken from her—essentially forcing Joan back into men's clothing and violating her promise to not "cross-dress." Below is an excerpt from the trial documents after the recantation of her abjuration:

> JOAN: "I have but now resumed the dress of a man and put off the woman's dress."
>
> JUDGES: "Why did you take it, and who made you take it?"
>
> JOAN: "I took it of my own free will, and with no constraint: I prefer a man's dress to a woman's dress."
>
> JUDGES: "You promised and swore not to resume a man's dress."
>
> JOAN: "I never meant to swear that I would not resume it."
>
> JUDGES: "Why have you resumed it?"
>
> JOAN: "Because it is more lawful and suitable for me to resume it and to wear man's dress, being with men, than to have a woman's dress. I have resumed it because the promise made to me has not been kept; that is to say, that I should go

to Mass and should receive my Saviour and that I should be taken out of irons."

JUDGES: "Did you not abjure and promise not to resume this dress?"

JOAN: "I would rather die than be in irons! but if I am allowed to go to Mass, and am taken out of irons and put into a gracious prison, and may have a woman for companion, I will be good, and do as the Church wills."[i]

Joan's testimony shows that she may not have been aware of what she had sworn to, but it served its purpose. With it, Cauchon could argue that Joan was inconsistent and still a heretic despite her abjuration, and he ordered her execution for May 30, 1431.

The Execution of Joan of Arc

On the morning of May 30, 1431, Joan received special permission from Bishop Cauchon to make her final confession and receive communion ahead of her execution. She was led by a pair of Dominican priests to Place du Vieux-Marché, in the center of Rouen. There, she was handed over to the secular military authorities, who led her to a pyre that had been constructed for her execution. Her sentence and a sermon of her heresy were read aloud, and by all accounts, Joan was distraught as she was bound to the plaster pillar on top of the pyre. She called upon the saints she was familiar with for guidance and was apparently so moving that even her enemies found themselves with tears in their eyes. An English soldier and Dominican priest each took pity on her. One handed her a small wooden cross, which she wore around her neck, and the other held a large crucifix aloft so she could focus on the icon and pray. With her last breath, she cried out to Jesus before succumbing to the fire. Until the end, she maintained that her visions and voices were divine in nature and affirmed her piety and faith in the Catholic Church.

Officially, Joan of Arc died of smoke inhalation, and the officials who executed her had to burn her body three times before it completely turned to ash. In the ensuing years, the executioner claimed to have felt eternally damned for his role in executing a holy woman.

---

[i] Søren Bie, "Second Process: The Relapse, The Final Adjudication, and The Sentence of Death. Jeanne D'Arc La Pucelle, accessed June 24, 2024, https://www.jeanne-darc.info/trial-of-condemnation-index/trial-condemnation-second-process-the-relapse-adjudication-and-death-sentence/.

The English and Burgundian forces had hoped to rally their troops against Joan to discredit her and make the French lose faith in their heroine, but her execution proved to have the opposite effect. Those in attendance were reassured of her faith, and her death gave the French troops the resolve to continue fighting for their land.

Why Was Joan of Arc Burned at the Stake?

It is common to think burning a woman at the stake was reserved for the accusation of witchcraft, but there were other, more political reasons to have executed Joan of Arc in such a brutal, public display. For one, her trial and execution were as much a show as a criminal procedure. The forces of King Henry VI knew how popular Joan of Arc was, and they knew word of her execution would spread. (But this opened the door for misinformation and conspiracy, as well.) They needed to execute her publicly so that no one could refute their claims that they had stopped the heroine in her tracks. They wanted to use the opportunity as a show of military force, not only a religious decree.

Political Aftermath — End of War

Charles VII is said to have been devastated to hear of Joan's execution. He was already trying to make peace with his Burgundy foes, and in 1435—four years after Joan's execution—the Burgundians and Armagnac (French) forces finally reconciled under the crown of Charles VII with the Treaty of Arras. This helped unify French alliances against the English and was a significant turn in the tide of the war. With no allies on the mainland, the English began to lose their hold in Northern France and experienced a steady decline in power. The Hundred Years' War would continue to rage on for another twenty-two years until the Battle of Castillon in 1453 when the French won a decisive victory over the English forces, driving them back to Calais and reclaiming all their territory.

Aftermath of the Execution

The initial campaign to brand Joan a heretic did affect the people of France. But, gradually, the perception of Joan's military successes and the trial began to shift. As time passed, people began to question the fairness of the trial and the validity of its outcome. Her role in the military victories of France replaced the doubt sowed by the English, and she slowly transformed into the symbol of French resistance we know today. Since her success on the battlefield had already begun to wane, it can be argued that her trial and execution paved the way for her legend, rather than sinking Joan into history as a forgotten (or disliked) military leader.

Rehabilitation Effort

The effort to clear Joan's name and reverse the accusations made against her at trial did not formally begin until almost twenty years after her death. Her mother, Isabelle Romée, was a major factor in the campaign. However, in the early years post-execution, the war got in the way of her personal efforts as she moved from Domrémy to Orléans after her husband's death.

She was not the only one who hoped to clear Joan's name only to be delayed by the war. Charles VII knew it was unfavorable that someone declared a "relapsed heretic" had crowned him as king—especially when the battle for the French crown had gone on for so long. His desire to rehabilitate Joan's public image had to wait until Rouen—the city where the initial trial took place and all the trial documents were located—was no longer under English rule. Finally, in 1449, Rouen fell to Charles' forces, and he could begin to think seriously about appealing the ruling against Joan.

By 1450, the English had been driven back to Normandy, and Charles VII was secure on the French throne with his former Burgundian enemy, Philip the Good, on his side. Charles VII was determined to stay in power. He ordered the University of Paris to review its initial judgment and investigate any abuses that may have occurred during the trial, but the university was reluctant to do so since many of its members had been participants. While they had changed sides in the years since the trial, they did not want to risk any retaliation that may happen if they were found guilty of abuse in judgment. The university's reluctance, along with a surge in the war that consumed Charles VII's attention, led to a halt in the proceedings. They would be placed on the back burner for another two years.

The case was taken up again in 1452 by Cardinal Guillaume d'Estouteville, an aristocratic bishop from Normandy who was anxious to prove his loyalty to Charles VII's reign. He began to collect testimony in Joan's favor but was ultimately encouraged to turn the investigation over to a secular leader so as not to conflict with the Catholic Church. D'Estouteville passed the investigation on to the Inquisitor-General, Jean

Bréhal, who began to visit the cities and towns most familiar to Joan to collect the testimonies of those who knew her.

Finally, in 1455, with the help of Jean Bréhal, Isabelle Romée petitioned the newly appointed Pope Callixtus III to appeal the case against her daughter and review whether the trial was a just one under ecclesiastical law. She traveled to Paris to the newly constructed Notre Dame Cathedral for the official start of the appeal, along with her two sons and a cohort of friends.

1455 Nullification Trial

The following is Isabelle Romée's appeal:

> "I had a daughter born in lawful wedlock who grew up amid the fields and pastures. I had her baptized and confirmed and brought her up in the fear of God. I taught her respect for the traditions of the Church as much as I was able to do given her age and simplicity of her condition. I succeeded so well that she spent much of her time in church and after having gone to confession she received the sacrament of the Eucharist every month. Because the people suffered so much, she had a great compassion for them in her heart and despite her youth she would fast and pray for them with great devotion and fervor. She never thought, spoke or did anything against the faith. Certain enemies had her arraigned in a religious trial. Despite her disclaimers and appeals, both tacit and expressed, and without any help given to her defense, she was put through a perfidious, violent, iniquitous and sinful trial. The judges condemned her falsely, damnably and criminally, and put her to death in a cruel manner by fire. For the damnation of their souls and in notorious, infamous and irreparable loss to me, Isabelle, and mine. I demand that her name be restored."[i]

The nullification trial officially began on November 7, 1455, in Paris, and it marked a major turning point in the perception of Joan of Arc. The court meticulously examined the flaws and inconsistencies of the original trial and gathered extensive testimony about Joan's character,

---

[i] Søren Bie, "Jean D'Arc's Trial of Nullification 1455," In *Jean d'Arc Maid of Orleans Deliverer of France*, edited by Douglass Murray (1902), Jeanne d'Arc la pucelle, accessed June 24, 2024, https://www.jeanne-darc.info/trial-of-nullification/.

lifelong piety, and religious commitment, enabling them to clear her name and lay the groundwork for her enduring legacy. The nullification trial declared that the original trial was invalid due to bias and procedural errors, and the court annulled the verdict.

Timeline of the Nullification Trial

1450 - Initial Inquiry:

- In March, Guillaume Bouillé, a theologian at the University of Paris, conducts an initial inquiry into Joan's original trial in Rouen, interviewing seven witnesses. This inquiry was ordered by King Charles VII to investigate the faults and abuses of the original trial.

1452 - Further Investigation:

- Cardinal Guillaume d'Estouteville and Jean Bréhal, the Inquisitor of France, conduct a more comprehensive investigation into Joan's trial. This investigation involved gathering testimonies and examining the procedural errors and biases that had tainted the original trial.

June 1455 - Authorization of the Retrial:

- Pope Callixtus III issues a papal declaration authorizing a new trial to be overseen by three papal commissioners, with Joan's surviving family as plaintiffs. This decision was influenced by the findings of the earlier investigations conducted by d'Estouteville and Bréhal.

November 7, 1455 - Opening of the Retrial:

- The nullification trial officially opens at Notre Dame Cathedral in Paris. The trial is attended by a large crowd, including Joan's family. The venue later shifts to the episcopal court of Paris.

January-May 1456 - Gathering Testimonies:

- January-February 1456: Thirty-four witnesses are heard in Domrémy and Vaucouleurs.
- February-March 1456: Forty-one witnesses are heard in Orléans.
- April-May 1456: Twenty witnesses are heard in Paris.
- December 1455 and May 1456: Nineteen witnesses are heard in Rouen.

- May 28, 1456: Jean d'Aulon's deposition is taken in Lyon.

June 1456 - Final Summary:
- Jean Bréhal completes his final summary ("Recollectio") of the case, which forms the basis for the final judgment.

July 7, 1456 - Final Verdict:
- The court declares Joan innocent, nullifying the original verdict. The judges state that the twelve articles on which Joan was condemned were drafted "corruptly, deceitfully, slanderously, fraudulently, and maliciously." Joan's sentence is declared null and void, and a cross is ordered to be erected at the spot in Rouen where she died.

Joan's Legacy Post-Nullification

The nullification trial officially reversed the heresy charge, changing Joan's execution into a martyrdom since she suffered and died for her religious beliefs. This cemented her legacy as a hero in both the Catholic and military worlds and secured support for the legitimacy of Charles VII's reign. Since he was coronated by a martyr, and not a condemned heretic, there was no reason for anyone to contest the validity of Charles VIII's claim to the French crown. Since Joan was considered a martyr, this opened the path for her eventual canonization, which would happen almost five hundred years after her death. Most significantly, the trial—and the publicity surrounding it—reinforced Joan's image as a national heroine in France, a symbol of patriotism and resistance, and an icon of the divine.

One of the most important and understated impacts of the trial is the wealth of historical information we now have about Joan's life. The nullification trial included testimony about her childhood in Domrémy, all the eyewitness accounts that were interviewed, and their testimonies recorded by Bréhal. This trove is rare for a medieval figure who was not a member of the noble class and gives historians a glimpse into what peasant life was like in fourteenth-century France.

Chapter 8 – Sainthood

Joan of Arc's legacy surpassed her brief life thanks to the work her family and admirers did to ensure she would be remembered as the remarkable woman she was. They began with her trial, working to reverse the damage done by the British and nullify her guilt; next, they began the arduous process of remembering Joan of Arc as a saint, a martyr, and a divine woman. The road to sainthood was not an easy one. It was not until 1920—almost five hundred years after her death—that she was canonized as a saint in the Catholic Church. During that time, the image and memory of Joan of Arc changed but never faded, growing in veneration in the minds of the French people and Catholics across the world.

Timeline of Sainthood

- 1869: The process for Joan's beatification began under Pope Pius IX.
- January 27, 1894: Pope Leo XIII declared Joan of Arc "Venerable," recognizing her heroic virtues.
- April 11, 1909: Pope Pius X beatified Joan of Arc, acknowledging her as "Blessed Joan of Arc."
- January 6, 1919: Pope Benedict XV announced the canonization process for Joan of Arc.
- May 16, 1920: Joan of Arc was canonized as a saint by Pope Benedict XV in a ceremony at St. Peter's Basilica in Rome.

- <u>1922</u>: Pope Pius XI declared Joan of Arc one of the patron saints of France along with the Virgin Mary, Saint Michael the Archangel, and Saint Louis, solidifying her status as a national symbol and spiritual protector of the country.

Canonization

Canonization, in the Roman Catholic Church, is the process by which a person becomes recognized as a saint and becomes eligible for veneration. It is a rigorous process that signifies a person who has been recognized as a model of faith, hope, and charity throughout their extraordinary life. The process begins with a petition from a local leader, typically a bishop, followed by a thorough investigation into the candidate's life and virtues. The goal of canonization is to confirm that a person has lived a life that demonstrated extraordinary virtues and intervened in miracles after their death, making them worthy of sainthood and designation as role models for those who ascribe to the Catholic faith.

Contrary to what you may believe, the process of canonization is strict and informed by both theological and scientific investigation. With a few rare exceptions, the process can only begin at least five years after the candidate's death.

Process of Canonization

There are three different stages in the process of canonization, with four titles that the candidate receives on the road to sainthood:

PHASES	STEPS	DESCRIPTION
Diocean	Initial Petition and Nihil Obstat Decree	The process begins with an initial petition either to or by the bishop of the diocese where the candidate died, requesting the case for canonization. If the bishop approves, he will go to the Holy See (the office of the pope) to obtain a "Nihil Obstat" (Latin, "Nothing Hinders") decree, which makes sure there are no doctrinal or moral impediments to investigating the life, virtues, and sanctity of the candidate. If the Holy See approves

PHASES	STEPS	DESCRIPTION
		and the decree is obtained, the process may begin.
	"Servant of God"	Once the initial petition is approved and the process is allowed to begin, the candidate is then referred to as "Servant of God." The title emphasizes their devotion to God and their role as a faithful servant of the divine and signifies that they lived a life of "extraordinary virtue."
	Diocean Investigation and Positio	The local Diocese gathers a tribunal to conduct an extensive investigation into the candidate's life and virtues. They gather all this information in a document called the "Positio," a comprehensive summary prepared by the Diocesan Tribunal for the Congregation of the Causes of Saints in Rome. The Positio includes the candidate's biography, a description of their heroic and theological virtues, an account of all miracles attributed to them, testimony of witnesses, and any other written records that would support the case for canonization. The Positio is the basis for the Congregation's evaluation of the candidate's virtues and the main body of support for canonization.
Roman	Congregation for the Causes of Saints Investigates	The Congregation for the Causes of Saints reviews the Positio and conducts its own investigation, verifying the claims within. Members of the Holy See vote on whether the candidate lived a heroic life. If the majority is in favor, the cause is passed on to the

PHASES	STEPS	DESCRIPTION
		cardinals and bishops for further evaluation.
	"Venerable"	If the candidate is declared Venerable, it means that the pope has recognized their heroic virtues. This stage is a significant milestone in the process as it indicates that the candidate is now eligible for beatification.
Beatification and Canonization	Verification of the First Miracle	Before beatification, the Church requires evidence of at least four miracles attributed to the intercession of the Venerable. This involves scientific and theological evaluations to confirm that the miracles have no natural explanation.
	Beatification	Beatification is the second-to-last stage in the canonization process. It is a formal declaration by the pope that the Venerable is now a Blessed. This means they are considered to be in heaven and are worthy of veneration by the faithful. To be beatified, the Blessed must have one miracle attributed to their intercession, which is verified by the Congregation for the Causes of Saints. During the beatification ceremony, the pope issues a formal declaration, and the candidate is given the title "Blessed" (Latin: "Beatus"). The ceremony typically involves a mass, prayers, and the veneration of the Blessed's relics. Beatification is a significant milestone, as it marks the first official recognition of the

PHASES	STEPS	DESCRIPTION
		Blessed's sainthood by the Church.
	Verification of the Second Miracle	Similar to the verification of miracles before beatification, the Congregation for the Causes of Saints requires evidence of a new miracle, one that occurs after the declaration of "Blessed." As with the first verification, theological and scientific experts evaluate to confirm the miracle has no natural explanation.
	Canonization Decree	Once the final miracle is confirmed, the pope can declare the candidate's sainthood, marking the final stage in the process. The Canonization Decree is a solemn announcement that officially declares that the candidate has ascended to heaven, is an intercessory for the living, and is worthy of universal veneration. The pope will usually deliver a speech stating the candidate's virtues and the miracles attributed to them during the canonization process. The occasion is marked by a ceremonial mass and other celebrations.

Not all candidates make it through to sainthood. If the Congregation for the Causes of Saints or the pope (Holy See) decides the criteria for a given stage are not met, they will halt the process. The candidate will be remembered with the title they acquired unless an issue arises within the process.

Bishop Félix Dupanloup of Orléans and His Petition

Joan of Arc's canonization began with the efforts of Bishop Félix Dupanloup of Orléans. Dupanloup was a prominent figure in Liberal Catholicism, a bishop, and an educator who became the Bishop of Orléans in 1849, a position he held until his death in 1878. As Bishop of Orléans, Dupanloup advocated for educational freedom and defended the Catholic Church during the time of Napoleon. Dupanloup saw Joan's value as a unifying figure. At this point in history, her story was being re-examined, and Dupanloup likely took advantage of the new scholarship to restore her reputation.

In 1849, Dupanloup delivered a panegyric (tribute) on Joan of Arc and began his campaign to promote her to sainthood. He spent the next twenty years investigating Joan's cause and collecting testimony to create his petition to canonize her, finally presenting his case to Pope Pious IX in 1869. With the support of the Diocese of Orléans, Joan was elevated to "Servant of God." In 1894, Pope Pious IX officially initiated the process of canonization, presenting her case to the Sacred Congregation for the Causes of Saints.

Beatification of Joan of Arc

The Sacred Congregation conducted their investigation into Joan's life and death, including historical documents, eyewitness accounts, and a review of her two trials. Though the "crimes" from her initial trial were nullified, that trial was less public than the first. So, while Joan's image had been rehabilitated, the accusations of heresy from the first trial were still in the public consciousness. The road to sainthood did not run smoothly, with members of the Congregation citing her capture as evidence that she was not in communion with God, doubting her feminine purity, and rejecting the initial proposal to add Joan of Arc to the calendar of saints.

Eventually, Pope Pious X approved the promotion of Joan to the status of "Venerable" and then began the process of validating miracles associated with Joan of Arc to beatify her. Typically, one needs four miracles to be considered "Blessed" unless a religious order is founded in that person's honor. In Joan's case, Pope Pious X (the successor to Pious IX, who started Joan's petition) declared that, as the savior of

France, Joan already had one of these miracles under her belt. While she did not start a religious order, she was already an almost mythical figure in the eyes of the French and had led their military to victory at Orléans thanks to her communion with God. Finally, in 1909, Pope Pious X declared Joan of Arc a "Blessed," recognizing her piety, heroic virtues, and martyrdom.

Janvier's Pantograph

At around the same time, Victor Janvier was working on an improved die engraving machine, intended at first for sculptors to be able to reduce the size of their creations. His machine, named the Janvier Pantograph, was patented merely ten years before Joan of Arc's beatification and

went on to become useful as a coin-minting press. By 1921, it was being used in the national mint of twenty-four countries around the world.

By 1909, when Joan was finally raised to the status of Blessed, the machine was being used commercially to create commemorative medallions and coins, resulting in a series of medals featuring scenes from Joan's life. This added to the already popular canon of art featuring Joan of Arc and made it so that anyone could keep a piece of her in their pocket. She was no longer exclusive to grand paintings in museums or small bronze sculptures at home. Anyone who wished to pray over Joan or carry her likeness with them for courage could do so with a simple coin in their pocket.

Canonization of Joan of Arc

The process of canonization was interrupted by the First World War, during which Joan of Arc's popularity experienced a renaissance in France. French troops, enabled by new commercial presses like the Janvier Pantograph, brought her image with them into the trenches, and Joan became a renewed symbol of French resistance for a new generation. At one point during the war, French soldiers interpreted an image of a German searchlight projected onto low-lying clouds as an appearance by Joan, boosting their morale in battle.

Her legend crossed the Atlantic into the United States, as well. In 1918, a poster featuring Joan of Arc was used in the US to encourage women to buy war bonds to support their country. She was even featured in a musical. The song "Joan of Arc, They Are Calling You" was featured in the musical *This Way Out* in 1917, with lyrics crying out for Joan's guidance amid the deadliest war the world had ever seen. The chorus is as follows:

> "Joan of Arc, Joan of Arc,
>
> Do your eyes, from the skies, see the foe?
>
> Don't you see the drooping Fleur-de-lis?
>
> Can't you hear the tears of Normandy?
>
> Joan of Arc, Joan of Arc,
>
> Let your spirit guide us through;
>
> Come lead your France to victory;
>
> Joan of Arc, they are calling you. Joan of you."[i]

Soon after the war was over, in 1920, Pope Benedict XV officially canonized Joan of Arc as a saint in the Catholic Church, naming May 30 as her feast day. Over thirty thousand people—including some of her descendants—attended the canonization ceremony, which took place at St. Peter's Basilica in Rome.

The canonization ceremony for Joan of Arc.[16]

---

[i] Jack Wells, Alfred Bryan, and Willie Weston, "Joan of Arc They Are Calling You," Digital Commons at Connecticut College Historic Sheet Music Collection, 1917, https://digitalcommons.conncoll.edu/sheetmusic/777.

Pope Pius XI's Speech about Her Canonization (1922):

"Regarding the Maid of Orleans that Our predecessor elevated to the supreme honor of the saints, nobody can question whether under the auspices of the Virgin that she has received and fulfilled the mission of saving France, for First, it is under the patronage of Our Lady of Bermont, then under that of the Virgin of Orleans, and finally the Virgin of Reims, she undertook a manly heart so much work, that She remained fearless in the face with swords unsheathed and spotless in the midst of the license camps, she freed his country from the supreme peril and restored the fortunes of France. After having received the advice of his heavenly voice she added on her glorious banner of the name Mary of Jesus, the true King of France. Mounted on the stake, it is whispering in flames in a final scream, the names of Jesus and Mary, she flew to heaven. So, having experienced the obvious relief of the Maid of Orleans, that France receives the favor of the second heavenly patron: it demanding that the clergy and people, which was already better in our predecessor and we are pleased to Ourselves.

Therefore, after taking the advice of our venerable brothers the cardinals of the Holy Roman Church attendants Rites motu proprio, With certain knowledge and after careful deliberation, in the fullness of our apostolic power, by force of the present and in perpetuity, We declare and confirm that the Virgin Mary Mother of God under the title of her Assumption into heaven, has been regularly chosen as the principal patron of all France with God, with all the privileges and honors that include the noble title and dignity.

Furthermore, listening to the wishes of pressing bishops, clergy and faithful of the dioceses and missions of France, we declare with the greatest joy and establish the illustrious Maid of Orleans, especially admired and revered by all Catholics France as the heroine of religion and the homeland, St. Jeanne d'Arc, virgin, secondary patroness of France, selected by the full vote of the people, and it even after our supreme apostolic authority, also granting all the honors and privileges under the law includes this as a second patron.

Accordingly, we pray God, the author of any property that, by the intercession of two celestial patrons, the Mother of God assumed into Heaven and St. Jeanne d'Arc, virgin, and other patron saints of places and holders churches, dioceses that both missions, Catholic France, hopes strained towards true liberty and its ancient dignity, is really the first-born daughter of the Roman Church, it warms, guard, developed by thinking, action, love, its ancient and glorious traditions for the good of religion and the homeland.

We grant these privileges, determining that these letters are still firm and remain valid and effective, that they obtain and retain their full force and effect, both now and in the future for the entire French nation, the pledge broader relief heavenly way it should be judged definitively, and that is now held vain and void for future development which would adversely affect these decisions, because of any authority either knowingly or unknowingly. Notwithstanding anything to the contrary. (Given at Rome, at St. Peter, under the seal of the Fisherman, the 2nd of March of 1922, the first of Our Pontificate years.)"[i]

Reactions to Saint Joan

Two years after her canonization, St. Jeanne d'Arc was named the patron saint of France, and the French declared May 8 to be a national holiday in her honor. By the time of her canonization, the accusations made against her at trial were long dismissed to history, and she had been revived as a symbol of French resistance and resilience. Later, during World War II, her image would once again be used to boost morale, not only in France but also all over the Allied world. Overall, there were no major negative reactions to the canonization of Joan.

---

[i] Søren Bie, "Canonization of Jeanne d'Arc," Jeanne d'arc la pucelle, March 16, 2016, https://www.jeanne-darc.info/biography/canonization.

A lithograph of an American poster promoting stamps.[17]

Chapter 9 – A Lasting Legacy

Pope Benedict XV finally made Joan of Arc a saint in 1920, but it did not take the Catholic Church to beatify her in history. As a female leader in war, she joins a rank bestowed upon few women throughout history and has been remembered as a national figure in France since her death. Her legacy persists beyond history into art, literature, and society, making her an inspiration to young women in the modern age—far beyond her religious reach.

The Portrayal of Joan of Arc

Joan of Arc's portrayal across art, literature, and theater has been remarkably diverse, reflecting the multifaceted nature of her legacy. She is much more than her sainthood and more nuanced than a military leader. Her story blends history with legend to the point where she can be interpreted more as a mythical figure than a historical one. Joan of Arc has been depicted by countless artists, spanning numerous artistic movements, and each artist has focused on different parts of her legacy.

Joan in Literature, Theater, and Film

Joan's life has been depicted since the fifteenth century, first in literature with Christine de Pizan's elegiac poem, "Chanson en l'honneur de Jeanne d'Arc," and most recently with *Joan of Arc: Into the Fire*, a musical written by Talking Heads frontman David Byrne. He describes her story as such:

> "Why has this story endured over centuries and been made into so many plays and movies? Because it's about

someone—a nobody, a teenage girl—who inspired others to act, to overthrow their oppressors and take charge of their lives. She transforms from an innocent, into an androgynous warrior, and finally a martyr. Joan's story is about the power of the individual to make a difference and (for me) the hubris and sometimes oversteps that often go along with that. In other words—it's completely relevant."[i]

On Screen...

Theater and cinema offer a unique perspective on the legacy of Saint Joan. Her depictions in film show us that the story of Joan of Arc is so relevant that it does not even need to be anchored in medieval France for audiences to immediately understand and connect to the story.

In 1928, Carl Theodor Dryer directed *The Passion of Joan of Arc*, which is noted for its use of extreme close-ups of Joan of Arc's haunted expression at her trial. Dreyer's film, with its minimalist approach, captures the spiritual and emotional intensity of Joan's trial. He felt he did not need to use historically accurate clothes or sets—or sound!—because, to him, the story of Joan is the story of her spirit and passion. As he said, "The year of the event seemed as inessential to me as its distance from the present. I wanted to interpret a hymn to the triumph of the soul over life."[ii]

Her story has been adapted to the setting of World War I (*Joan the Woman*, directed by Cecil B. DeMille), as well as faithfully depicted within her time period. Directors like Victor Fleming emphasize her heroic dimensions and the tragedy of her story, while more modern adaptations, such as Luc Besson's film *The Messenger*, focus on Joan as a psychologically complex figure, driven by visions and trauma.

She has been portrayed by famous actresses such as Geraldine Farrar, Ingrid Bergman (who played her twice, once in English and once in France), Jean Seberg, and Milla Jovovich—all actresses who have been noted for individualistic performances and their portrayals of strong women.

---

[i] Matthew Strauss, "David Byrne Wrote a Musical About Joan of Arc," *Pitchfork*, May 19, 2016, pitchfork.com/news/65596-david-byrne-wrote-a-musical-about-joan-of-arc/.

[ii] "*Sight & Sound* Poll 2012: *The Passion of Joan of Arc*," *The Criterion Collection*, September 18, 2012, www.criterion.com/current/posts/2475-sight-sound-poll-2012-the-passion-of-joan-of-arc.

These pieces examine her legacy from many different perspectives, some focusing on her heroism, some on the feminist nature of her life, and others on the psychological nature of her visions. These diverse portrayals reflect a story that is continually inspiring and perpetually relevant.

Poster for The Passion of Joan of Arc starring Maria Falconetti.[18]

Poster for Saint Joan starring Jean Seberg.[19]

...And Stage

On stage, her story has been adapted into numerous plays, from Friedrich Schiller's romantic tragedy *The Maid of Orleans* to George Bernard Shaw's more nuanced exploration of her character in *Saint Joan*.

Shaw's depiction of Joan of Arc in *Saint Joan* can be considered the first secular portrayal of the historical figure. While most other theatrical depictions are melodramatic and focus on her religious significance, Shaw portrays her visions as examples of Joan's military genius rather than a divine connection, exploring the political motivations that surrounded the events of her life and leaning into questions of the gender norms, nationalism, and traditional authority of the period. Doing so allowed Shaw to use the play to express his philosophy and ideas.

Shaw wrote *Saint Joan* in 1923—three years after Joan was canonized as a saint and five years after the bloodbath of World War I—a war that began and ended with nationalism at its core. Shaw used the story of Joan of Arc to look back at wars of nationalism and what it meant to fight for your country. As we previously examined, the idea of a "national identity" did not exist before Joan of Arc and the Hundred Years' War. Before that, knights fought in the name of a lord. They may have fought petty battles for their land, but it was not until the Armagnacs, Burgundians, and the English that people became organized as a military and fought for their king and a unified "national" identity.

Shaw's version was the first to humanize the mythical figure and explore the more practical reasons and consequences of her life. It notably lacks a clear villain—a big departure for the time—and instead depicts characters acting within their historical context and reacting to the consequences of their actions. We cannot know for sure what Joan felt or thought during her life beyond what was said at her trial, but interpretations like this allow us to glimpse our world through her lens. By humanizing Joan, Shaw kept his text accessible to audiences, allowing them to think about how what they saw on stage related to their day-to-day life.

Joan of Arc: The Paintings

There are few depictions of the real Joan of Arc. There are no photographs or royal portraits of her, only descriptions of what she looked like and one small illustration, but that has not stopped artists from painting her. Joan of Arc and her battle against the English has been painted throughout the centuries, transcending artistic movements and trends. Each portrayal reflects the cultural and political climate of its time.

Her story has inspired countless visual interpretations, but there is generally a common theme throughout them—Joan is often depicted mid-battle, clad in armor, with her red hair draped behind her. How does this reflect what we know about Joan—that she was reported to dress in men's armor, with cropped hair that was considered masculine for the time? Do these depictions focus on her beauty to emphasize her divine nature or the extraordinariness of her life? While looking at the paintings, it is important to ask what the context behind the period and the painter was and how that might have influenced the depiction or interpretation of Joan.

In the Baroque period, the Flemish artist Peter Paul Rubens painted Joan of Arc kneeling at an altar, presumably as she prays for bravery in her fight against the English. Her gloved hands are unsheathed as she looks toward the figure of Jesus Christ on the cross. The two figures draw heavy parallels—both were holy figures who received divine communications with God, both were called by these divine communications to become leaders to a band of followers, and both were arrested and persecuted for their divine connections. Could this version of Joan be communicating with the spirit of Jesus Christ, searching for a holy connection between the two?

Rubens painted his Joan during a period of intense conflict between Catholics and Protestants in the Netherlands, so the painting can alternatively be interpreted as a veneration of a nationalistic, unifying figure during a time of conflict. In the painting, Joan is much larger than the ghostly figure of Jesus Christ, signifying either that Rubens found her to be more important or that her legend loomed over that of Jesus. But she still bows her head to him, showing her respect.

By contrast, in Sir John Everett Millais' painting (also titled *Joan of Arc*, painted in 1865), Joan is kneeling while holding her sword. Her armored hands are not knit in prayer, and she is the only visible figure. This painting is more secular, portraying Joan more humanly and comparing her to no one but herself. The Joan in Millais' Pre-Raphaelite painting is not a Catholic figure but a historical one—a

Joan of Arc by Peter Paul Rubens.[20]

woman who could be listening to divine voices or just as easily contemplating her military strategy.

A painting of Joan of Arc by Sir John Everett Millais.[21]

In the last painting, *Joan of Arc's Entrance into Orleans* by Jean-Auguste Dominique Ingres shows yet another side of Joan. This famous painting depicts Joan's entrance to Orléans, breaking the English siege. It is the least religious of the three paintings yet shows a common theme— Joan of Arc in silver armor. In this painting of Joan surrounded by the French army, marching through the streets as if guided by light, we still see some of the ecclesiastic elements from the other paintings. However, this portrayal is also tinted with a nationalistic fever. Joan is not alone; she is surrounded by the French people celebrating her victory. She is still saintly thanks to the light in her face, but she is also human.

Modern Depictions of Joan of Arc

Throughout the twentieth century and to the present day, Joan of Arc has continued to inspire artists, though their focus on her as a subject has changed. Post-canonization Joan of Arc is more than a saint; she is also a feminist figure, a figure of dreams and legend, and a story to inspire young children. Salvador Dali, in his characteristic surreal style, drew a Joan of Arc who is mid-battle (perhaps referencing the Impressionist Franck Craig's painting *Joan of Arc in Battle* from 1907). She is seemingly able to fly as if carried by her visions. In 2018, the artist Alex Tuzinsky created a painting in which Joan appears to be carried by her visions in a dream-like state. How will the interpretation of Joan of Arc change as her life moves farther away from us in history?

A painting of Joan of Arc in battle.[22]

Celebrating Joan of Arc: Festivals and Tourism

The memory of Joan is intrinsically tied to the national French identity. Her campaign against the English, along with the battle for France during the Hundred Years' War, is what originated a national "French" identity, so it follows that her life and legacy continue to be celebrated there today.

Jeanne, Johannique, La Pucelle

The three biggest festivals that celebrate Joan of Arc take place in the three major cities associated with her life—Orléans, Reims, and Vaucouleurs—though other, smaller festivals occur throughout France to celebrate the life of La Pucelle. The festivals typically take place during the first few weeks of May to coincide with the liberation of Orléans, her capture by the Burgundians, and the Coronation of Charles VII—as well as allow for outdoor festivals without the risk of bad weather.

Of these festivals, Les Fêtes de Jeanne d'Arc in Orléans has been taking place the longest. Its 595th edition was celebrated in May 2024. This festival consists of ten days in which various events pay tribute to Joan of Arc's story and legacy. It includes a procession through the streets that mimics the military liberation of Orléans, military and religious tributes to Saint Joan, markets, and concerts. The festival is the largest of its kind, in addition to being the longest-running, and expects large crowds every year to come learn about the legacy of Joan of Arc. In Reims and Vaucouleurs, re-enactments take the stage as the festivals focus more on the coronation of Charles VII and her expedition away from home to aid in his military campaign.

Nationalism and Far-Right Politics

In recent years, some Joan of Arc festivals (in particular, those taking place in Paris) have been marred by monarchist and far-right political movements that see Joan of Arc as a nationalist symbol of France. Her legacy indeed contributed to creating a unified French identity; however, some have co-opted this legacy with anti-republican and ultraconservative sentiments. Far-right groups like Action Française, Civitas, and National Rally have used her image in protests to support xenophobic ideals. Joan is a symbol of patriotism in France, but some would take this even further, claiming that she is a symbol only for those they consider truly "French." In this way, she is an example of how symbols of nationalism and patriotism can be co-opted and manipulated as time passes and stories are adapted.

Revisionist Views of Joan of Arc

Jeanne d'Arc existed over five hundred years ago, so it has been a long time since she has been able to tell her story in her own words. Over time, her legacy has been re-interpreted countless times through various lenses that provide insight into different parts of her story. As is common with medieval figures, historians have investigated texts and available records to re-examine what might have been true of her life and what belongs to her legend. In doing so, they offer us new points of view about her story that change as philosophy, politics, and history do.

A Feminist Icon

Joan of Arc did not have to wait long to be revered by both men and women in her lifetime. Thanks to Christine de Pizan, Joan was cemented in literature as an extraordinary woman—someone who dressed in men's clothes, cut her hair short, and rode a horse astride. She was an uncommon leader, and her figure would be adopted by other women throughout history who also felt they were uncommon.

The suffragettes in the early 1900s used Joan's image on a poster, dressing her in suffragette colors and having a woman dressed as Joan lead their protest marches through the streets. They were inspired by her story of rejecting masculine roles to pursue her calling. But was it a feminist calling if Joan herself would say it was religious? Joan's origins make the reinterpretation of her life as a feminist icon complicated. Joan would never have called herself a feminist. She responded to a higher calling outside of herself. But her memory has been adopted by those fighting for equality for women the same way it has been adopted as an icon of unity for France.

Additional, Lesser-known Theories About Joan of Arc

As one can see, there are many things about Joan's life that can be proven, traced, and fact-checked. At the same time, lesser-known and fascinating alternative theories regarding both her early life and her supposed later life also exist.

While it's important to note that the following are unproven theories, they still present an interesting window into the perception of Joan of Arc's story by some members of the general public, including those looking to exploit her life for their own needs and desires.

She Survived

One of the most frustrating things about society is that after a great tragedy, there will always be those willing to exploit it for their own gain. This type of opportunistic behavior comes in many forms. For instance, after a famous person dies, some con artists will claim to be the person thought to be dead. They always have an explanation of how this could be.

One of the most intriguing and false theories is that Joan of Arc was not burned at the stake. Instead, some have falsely theorized that a double was burned and that the real Joan lived a full life.

Shortly after Joan's very real execution, which was a public event with a large number of witnesses, an adventurer named Claude des Armoises (also known as Jeanne des Armoises) claimed to be Joan. Shockingly, that ruse worked for quite a while. Rather than accept some local fame and lead a quiet life with a famous name, Jeanne des Armoises chased fame and its spoils. Her con was said to be so good that as early as 1334, a mere three years after Joan's death, her actual brothers Pierre and Jean temporarily accepted Jeanne as the real Joan. While one might question how Joan's real brothers could be deceived in this way, it's important to keep in mind that grief can have a large effect on people. It's possible that her brothers really wanted to believe that she was their sister at the time.

However, even that was not good enough for the con artist. Over the next six years, Jeanne and her "brothers" toured France, during which time they visited Elisabeth von Görlitz, the widow of Prince Anton of Burgundy, and Princess Elizabeth of Luxembourg. All the while, "Joan" accepted gifts from admirers. As an example of her confidence in this scheme, this "come back tour" started at the site of one of Joan's greatest triumphs, Orléans, France.

However, as the saying goes, all good things must come to an end. In Jeanne's case, it happened when she dared to meet with Charles VII in Paris. During this meeting, the French monarch asked "Joan" to repeat a secret she had once told him years earlier. Unable to answer the question, Jeanne confessed to the lie and begged forgiveness. Unlike the real Joan, Jeanne was reportedly able to live out the rest of her days.

The 1870 book *Brewer's Dictionary of Phrase and Fable* by British author and Reverend E. Cobham Brewer sought to provide explanations on the origins of phrases and dispel myths surrounding historical events. Ironically, his book helped to muddy the waters of Joan of Arc's history.

In his book, Brewer claimed to have found evidence that Jeanne des Armoires was indeed Joan of Arc, though the evidence is flimsy at best. He claimed that a marriage document was found between a knight, Robert des Armoises, and a woman by the name of Jeanne, who bore the title "the Maid of Orléans." Brewer further points to documents showing payments to messengers in 1435 and 1436 from Joan to her brother John. He claimed that the real Joan and her husband, Robert des Armoises, lived at the Metz, where she put her past behind her and became a wife and mother.

While it's possible that the real Jeanne posed as Joan and later married and raised a family, there is far too much contradictory evidence for this theory to be true. As interesting as the story may be, the story of Jeanne des Armoires is just one example of someone attempting to take advantage of someone's untimely death. It's impossible to say how many others around that time attempted the same con.

She Was Secretly of Noble Blood

Another interesting and false theory regarding Joan involves her parentage. Some state she was the illegitimate child of Duke Louis of Orléans and Queen Isabeau of Bavaria. If this theory were true, which, to be clear, it is not, this would have made Joan the half-sister of Charles VII.

This particular theory seems to have taken shape around 1819 when French author Pierre Caze published *La Vérité sur Jeanne d'Arc* (*The Truth About Joan of Arc*). In his book, Caze theorizes that Joan was born out of a liaison between the two nobles, making her a bastard. Rather than dealing with the shame of such an affair, it was decided to give Joan to the d'Arc family to raise as their own. Apparently, Joan was even taught a private sign at some point in her early life. Upon meeting the future king, Charles VII, Joan would flash him the sign, which would prove that she was not a mere peasant but instead his half-sister.

While this theory is obviously false, some, including Caze himself, have used it to explain how Joan quickly gained Charles VII's trust. However, Joan's supposed father, Louis, died in 1407, five years before Joan's reported birth. There is literally no evidence to support the theory, though. Had there been, it's reasonable to assume that the idea would have gained the wide acknowledgment of historians and theologians.

One thing with outlandish theories such as this is that one or two truths usually remain, allowing the theory to grow. In this case, it is true that after Isabeau's husband, Charles VI, became very ill, the duke of Orléans became her constant companion. However, no intimate relationship between the two has been definitively proven. Though Queen Isabeau of Bavaria did give birth to a child in 1407, it was to a son named Philip, who unfortunately died in infancy. Perhaps Caze used this tragic death as a jumping-off point to come up with his theory of a mother using the death of a son as an opportunity to hide the story of a child born out of wedlock.

The Claim That Much of Her Life Was a Myth

Joan's short life was incredible. It was filled with more adventure and controversy than most people will experience, even if given longer lifespans. Yet, for all of the factual proof of her life and accomplishments, there have been those who have claimed that much of what is known about Joan of Arc is a myth.

Graeme Donald, an author who looks at historical misconceptions, claimed that there is a lack of evidence regarding Joan's life. Donald claims there are no portraits of her victories and no detailed accounts of her being in famous battles. Donald also states there was never any mention of Joan as a French military commander by 15th-century Burgundian chronicler and poet Georges Chastellain. As further proof to back up his theory, Donald claims that renowned French historian and archaeologist Jules Quicherat fabricated the events of her trials when he published his account between 1841 and 1849 after discovering documents that related to her trial. Jules Quicherat used what little real information he discovered to essentially create much of her history. Again, while this theory is potentially intriguing from a storytelling standpoint, it is just that—a theory.

Others, like 20th-century French writer Roger Caratini, claimed that Joan of Arc is based on propaganda rather than fact. His theory was that France at the time needed a hero, someone the nation could rally behind.

There is enough evidence to suggest that Joan of Arc was a real person and played a pivotal role in the war. However, Donald, Caratini, and others bring up solid points, as Joan of Arc's life isn't as well documented as, for instance, generals from that time period. Whether that was due to Joan of Arc being born a peasant or a woman or if it was because she didn't achieve as much as historians say, we will likely never know.

Chapter 10 – The Treatment of Other Women with Visions

Something to remember when thinking about Joan of Arc's incredible but all too short life is that she was not the first woman to experience visions. Not all of these women experienced the same treatment, and some are not known as widely as Joan. We have already spoken about Marie of Avignon, but let us take a look at Catherine of Siena and Bridget of Sweden. While both women died decades before Joan was born, the religious devotion displayed by both women made them hugely influential in their own right. But did they pay the price for following the path laid out by their visions as Joan of Arc did?

Catherine of Siena

In some ways, Catherine was very much like Joan in terms of her devotion to the Almighty. Born in Italy in 1347, shortly before the Black Death ravaged Europe, Catherine experienced her first vision at just six years old. Catherine was reported to have seen Christ alongside the apostles Peter, Paul, and John. Just a year later, young Catherine devoted her life to Christ. Throughout the rest of her life, Catherine continued to have visions where she communed with Jesus Christ and others.

As she grew, so did her dedication and her streak of independence. To avoid marrying her sister's widowed husband, Catherine cut her hair short in an act of defiance. Yet, despite such acts, she was devoted to helping others. Catherine was known to freely give away her family's food and clothing to those in need. She spent much of her life tending to and caring for the sick, and many began to see Catherine as a holy woman. Such work and dedication to helping others eventually led to Catherine having a dedicated group of followers, disciples of her very own. During her lifetime, she advocated for peace within Italy. She was instrumental in Pope Gregory IX's decision to return the papacy to Rome from Avignon, France, where it had been for decades.

Along with her political and missionary work, Catherine spread her message further by dictating letters to various scribes and secretaries. Her influence and voice were able to extend through the centuries due to the publication of a book called *The Dialogue of Saint Catherine of Siena*, which was finished in 1378. Even though she could read, the book's contents were dictated to her confessor and biographer, Raymond of Capua. This book and published letters to various leaders, including the pope, only helped cement her legacy and influence.

Unlike Joan, Catherine was able to live a relatively longer life, passing away at the age of thirty-three. While she was highly devoted to helping others, her dedication to her own faith took a tremendous physical toll on her body. Catherine was known to fast for long periods, including refusing to drink even water at one point. Unfortunately, this type of physical sacrifice resulted in her losing the use of her legs. Within a month of that happening, Catherine suffered a massive stroke, which paralyzed her from the waist down and played a part in her death.

In life, Catherine attracted a large and devoted following, much like Joan of Arc did. Also, like Joan, Catherine's influence grew in death. In fact, she was canonized just three decades after Joan's execution. Their circumstances were, of course, very different, but it is clear that Catherine did not face the same level of backlash at the time as her fellow future saint. She has long been regarded as someone spurred on by visions, and Italian literature focuses on her devotion to helping others.

Bridget of Sweden

Sweden's patron saint, Bridget of Sweden, experienced her first visions of Jesus Christ in 1309 at the age of seven. As one can expect, this experience helped to set the course of her life. Throughout the rest of her seventy years on earth, she continued to experience visions, including that of the nativity of Christ. Her description of this event greatly influenced artists' depictions of the nativity going forward.

Like Catherine and Joan, Bridget's life was devoted to helping others, both within and outside her community. At the age of thirteen, she married her husband, eighteen-year-old Prince Ulf Gudmarsson, the Swedish prince of Nericia. After that, she joined the Third Order of Saint Francis.

She and her new husband dedicated resources to building a hospital and caring for the needs of the poor. Bridget's religious devotion only strengthened in the years following her husband's death in 1341. Sometime later, Bridget received a vision telling her to find a new religious order. This vision became real when the Order of the Holy Savior, later known as the Bridgettines, was founded around 1346. Then, in 1351, during the height of the black plague, Bridget, along with several priests, disciples, and her daughter, who eventually became Saint Catherine of Vadstena, embarked on a pilgrimage to Rome, where Bridget spent the majority of her later life. The pilgrimage was undertaken with the goals of helping those in need and convincing Pope Clement VI to abandon France and return the papacy to Rome. Bridget was outspoken regarding her views on problems within the Catholic Church. Like Catherine of Siena, Bridget was adamant that the power of the church had to return to Rome.

However, despite all of the good she did and attempted to do, Bridget faced her share of criticism from those who opposed her. In the decades following her death in 1373, 15th-century priest and theologian Martin Luther was perhaps her loudest critic, as he would claim that her visions were nothing more than ravings. However, unlike Joan, Bridget was never forced to endure a show trial or any form of imprisonment or execution for her actions that were inspired by her visions. Bridget was also unique compared to Joan and Catherine. At the time of her birth in 1303, Bridget was born to a very wealthy family, which even included some royal lineage on her mother's side. Bridget was also the mother of eight children.

When looking at the differences and similarities between Joan of Arc, Catherine of Siena, and Bridget of Sweden, it is worth considering the life experiences Joan was robbed of due to her life being taken at such a young age. Would she have eventually married and had children? Who is to say?

Margery Kempe

Margery Kempe's story of religious devotion is fascinating in many ways. Unlike Bridget of Sweden or Catherine of Siena, Margery was alive during Joan of Arc's life, passing away less than a decade after Joan's execution. Like the women already mentioned, Margery was an extremely pious woman who experienced visions, which would play a large role in shaping the rest of her life.

Born around 1373 in Bishop's Lynn, England, Margery was the daughter of an English merchant and eventual member of Parliament, John Brunham. Little information exists about her early life, but she married businessman John Kemp, with whom she had fourteen children. While Margery was raised with a firm belief in the Almighty, she experienced her first visions in her twenties. As time went on, Margery's visions included her communicating with Jesus Christ, Mary, and God.

To show her religious devotion, she wore a clothing item known as a hair shirt, which was what it sounds like. Hair shirts were made from animal hair or coarse material. They were worn close to the skin. A hair shirt was to act as a form of wearable penance. In addition, Margery went to confession several times a day and even requested that her marriage to John become a marriage of chastity. It did not take long for word to spread about what many considered Margery's extreme religious devotion. Sadly, not everyone appreciated her approach to religion. This feeling of frustration grew within others when Margery began the habit of openly sobbing, wailing, and writhing as she begged God's forgiveness for a sin she committed.

Margery was brought up on charges of heresy several times. Her charges included things such as preaching as a woman and wearing all white as a married woman. Clearly, none of these charges were on the same level as those brought against Joan. Margery was never convicted for alleged crimes of heresy; she was jailed by priests and even threatened with assault for what could have been considered a vigorous form of worship.

Throughout her lifetime, Margery took several religious pilgrimages. Her first was to Jerusalem, but she also went to Santiago de Compostela in Spain and Prussia. These pilgrimages were inspired by Bridget of Sweden's pilgrimages after Margery heard a reading of an English translation of Briget's book.

Much of what we know about Margery came from her book, *The Book of Margery Kempe*. This book is considered by many to be the first autobiography written in the English language. She details her life, travels, and relationship with God in the book. However, there are some glaring historical omissions from the book. Despite the fact that she lived during the Hundred Years' War, the book makes no mention of the conflict or even the black plague that ravaged Europe.

Margery Kempe's story shows the personal sacrifices one is willing to make for one's own religious devotion and how she received unfair treatment based primarily on her gender. Had she been a man, it is arguable she might not have received so much pushback from society.

Conclusion

XXXIII

"Oh! How evident this was At Orleans, during the siege And when her strength had first appeared. No miracle, as I believe, Was ever clearer, for God helped His own so much, our foe could not Assist himself more than a dead Dog could; he died upon the spot."

XXXIV

"Aha!! What honor for the female Sex! God shows how he loves it, When the nobles—great, but wretched— Who earlier the realm had quit, By one woman were fortified, No men could do this deed, but more: The traitors were repaid in kind! No one would credit this before."

XXXV

"A girl of only sixteen years (Does this not outdo Nature's skill?) Who lightly heavy weapons bears, Of strong and hard food takes her fill, And thus is like it. And God's foes Before her swiftly fleeing run, She did this in the public eye. There tarried not a single one."

XXXVI

"She frees France from its enemies, Recovering citadels and castles. No army ever did so much, Not even a hundred thousand vassals! And of our brave and able folk, She is the chief and first commander. God makes it so; not even Hector Nor Achilles could withstand her."

— Christine de Pizan, *Le Ditié de Jehanne d'Arc*[i]

Joan's life, brief as it was, is a testament to the power of conviction and faith. Her visions, easily dismissed as the overactive imagination of a simple peasant girl, became the catalyst for a nation's resurgence and victory. Ultimately, this was because she was stubborn enough and certain in her mission. She had the bravery to do what the French military was previously afraid of—she took an offensive position rather than a defensive one and inspired her comrades to do the same.

The Siege of Orléans was broken in part thanks to her bravery and inspired leadership, making the turning point in a war that had become stagnant and that the French were at risk of losing completely. They were fighting like cowards, retreating farther south and trying desperately to defend their land, until Joan came along and inspired the opposite. Her unwavering belief in her divine mission blazed the trail for Charles VII's rightful coronation and encouraged him to begin the negotiations that would eventually rewrite the course of the Hundred Years' War.

Her story is not only one of military triumph. It is also a narrative that transcends the test of time and global borders and speaks to the capacity of the human spirit in the face of overwhelming odds. Not once did Joan question herself or bend to the will of those who wanted her to abandon her mission and become a political figurehead. The strength of her character and devotion unraveled a mockery of a trial, revealing the political and religious machinations behind it and making admirers of those who were prepared to hate her.

In the centuries that followed, her legacy grew far beyond that final trial, cementing Joan of Arc in the pantheon of heroes. Her posthumous exoneration and canonization contributed to that legacy, transforming her from a national hero into a symbol of empowerment and resistance.

Joan's life became a well of inspiration for artists, writers, and filmmakers who have taken different aspects of her life to use as lenses on our own. Each adds a new layer to her enduring myth, transforming her from a religious martyr to a ubiquitous figure representing bravery and hope. The new interpretations of her story help keep Joan of Arc in the collective consciousness as we relate to different parts of her story

---

[i] Christine de Pizan, *Ditié de Jeanne d'Arc*, ed. Angus J. Kennedy and Kennedy Varty (Oxford: Society for the Study of Medieval Languages and Literature 1977), trans. Leah Shopkow, https://dmdhist.sitehost.iu.edu/joan.htm

than before. Some have been inspired by Joan as an emblem for social change and gender equality, like the suffragettes of the early twentieth century or those who see her decision to dress in men's clothing as reaffirming their decision to live beyond the binaries of gender. It will be interesting to see how future generations interpret the story of Joan of Arc as they are born in an age where her legend has encompassed the realities of her life.

Joan's story is far from over. Her legend continues to transform as people see themselves in the many facets of her life and are inspired by her resistance. She is a symbol of unwavering conviction and a testament to the enduring power of an individual to change the course of history.

In this book, we have learned the basics of her life and only scratched the surface of the ways her life has inspired generations of artists. There is so much more to learn about the history around Joan of Arc.

One topic we were unable to delve deeper into was the Hundred Years' War—a complex and multifaceted struggle that involved shifting alliances and political machinations but revolved around competing claims to the French throne. Joan of Arc's role was pivotal in turning the tide of the war in favor of the French, but without the broader context, we are only seeing a porthole's worth of perspective into the war. The balance of power shifted multiple times throughout the Hundred Years' War, with both the English and French experiencing periods of dominance and setbacks. It also did not end with Edward III's dispute with Philip IV. The competition was sustained for generations as the kings of England and France fought to put their monarch on the throne before the other. The involvement of other European powers and conflicts, such as the influence of the Duchy of Burgundy and the Western Schism religious conflict, further complicated the geopolitical landscape and added to the complexity of the Hundred Years' War.

In addition, as the war progressed, the two countries relied less on feudalism and traditional chivalry and more on organized militaries. The fact that, by the end of the war, France had a somewhat organized military with a hierarchy we can recognize today also influenced the success that Joan of Arc had in lifting the Siege of Orléans and the conflicts along the Lorraine.

We were also unable to investigate the story of another influential woman of this time, Yolande of Aragon. As the mother-in-law of the Dauphin Charles VII, Yolande played a crucial role in supporting Joan of Arc and securing the resources and military support necessary for her mission. She was a skilled diplomat and political strategist who managed to navigate the treacherous political landscape of the time using her connections, influence, and sharp mind to bolster the French cause. Yolande's story provides valuable insights into the role of noblewomen and how they, too, shaped the course of the Hundred Years' War. Even in a male-dominated era, Yolande and Joan demonstrate the significant impact that women can have on the course of history.

By exploring alternate perspectives and the supporting figures around Joan of Arc's story, we can see how she fits into the larger tapestry of European history. It also helps us to understand why Joan's story has survived. But, for now, we have a better understanding of how Joan of Arc came to be the remarkable martyr we know today and why the memory of La Pucelle can be seen dotted all over France.

If you enjoyed this book, a review on Amazon would be greatly appreciated because it would mean a lot to hear from you.

To leave a review:
1. Open your camera app.
2. Point your mobile device at the QR code.
3. The review page will appear in your web browser.

Thanks for your support!

Here's another book by Enthralling History that you might like

Free limited time bonus

Stop for a moment. We have a free bonus set up for you. The problem is this: we forget 90% of everything that we read after 7 days. Crazy fact, right? Here's the solution: we've created a printable, 1-page pdf summary for this book that you're reading now. All you have to do to get your free pdf summary is to go to the following website: https://livetolearn.lpages.co/enthrallinghistory/

Or, Scan the QR code!

Once you do, it will be intuitive. Enjoy, and thank you!

Bibliography

Alizadeh, Alie. "The Maid Pictured: Truth and the Aesthetics of Joan of Arc." *NGV Triennial Voices*. Accessed July 6, 2024. https://www.ngv.vic.gov.au/exhibition_post/the-maid-pictured-truth-and-the-aesthetics-of-joan-of-arc/.

Berst, Charles A. "As Kingfishers Catch Fire: The Saints and Poetics of Shaw and T. S. Eliot." *Shaw* 14 (1994):105–25. https://www.jstor.org/stable/40655114.

Beyer, Greg. "Here's What Made Joan of Arc a French Heroine." *The Collector*, January 9, 2023. https://www.thecollector.com/what-made-joan-of-arc-french-heroine/.

Beyer, Greg. "Trial & Retrial: Joan of Arc's Death & What Happened to Her Body." *The Collector*, February 10, 2023. https://www.thecollector.com/joan-of-arc-death-trial/.

Bie, Søren. "Biography." Jeanne d'arc la pucelle, July 10, 2015. https://www.jeanne-darc.info/biography/.

Bie, Søren. "Canonization." Jeanne d'arc la pucelle, March 16, 2016. https://www.jeanne-darc.info/biography/canonization/.

Bie, Søren. "Jeanne d'Arc's Trial of Nullification 1455." Jeanne d'arc la pucelle. Accessed June 24, 2024. https://www.jeanne-darc.info/trial-of-nullification/.

Bie, Søren. "Locations and Battles of Jeanne d'Arc." Jeanne d'arc la pucelle, August 26, 2019. https://www.jeanne-darc.info/location/.

Bie, Søren. "Second Process: The Relapse, The Final Adjudication, and The Sentence of Death. Jeanne d'arc la pucelle. Accessed June 24, 2024.

https://www.jeanne-darc.info/trial-of-condemnation-index/trial-condemnation-second-process-the-relapse-adjudication-and-death-sentence/.

Bie, Søren. "The Attack on Paris." Jeanne d'arc la pucelle, June 17, 2018. https://www.jeanne-darc.info/location/paris/.

Bie, Søren, "The Chronology of Jeanne d'Arc." Jeanne d'arc la pucelle, July 10, 2015. https://www.jeanne-darc.info/biography/chronology/.

Bie, Søren. The Siege of Orléans (1428-1429)." Jeanne d'arc la pucelle, June 17, 2018. https://www.jeanne-darc.info/location/the-siege-of-orleans-1428-1429/.

Bie, Søren. "The Trial of Condemnation 1431." Jeanne d'arc la pucelle, February 14, 2016. https://www.jeanne-darc.info/trial-of-condemnation-index/.

Bounds, Joy. "Zabillet - the mother of Joan of Arc." *HerStoria Magazine*, July 29, 2012. https://www.herstoria.com/zabillet-the-mother-of-joan-of-arc/#After_Jehanne%E2%80%99s_death.

Bragg, Melvyn, host. In Our Time, "The Siege of Orléans." BBC Radio 4, May 24, 2007. Podcast, 45 minutes. https://www.bbc.co.uk/programmes/b007l3yq.

Britannica, T. Editors of Encyclopedia. "Félix-Antoine-Philibert Dupanloup." *Encyclopedia Britannica*, February 8, 2024. https://www.britannica.com/biography/Felix-Antoine-Philibert-Dupanloup.

Britannica, T. Editors of Encyclopedia. "Pierre Cauchon." *Encyclopedia Britannica*, February 21, 2024. https://www.britannica.com/biography/Pierre-Cauchon.

Bryan, Alfred and Weston, Willie. "Joan of Arc They Are Calling You." Waterson, Berlin, & Snyder Co., 1917. Library of Congress. Accessed July 6, 2024. https://www.loc.gov/resource/music.muswwism-200211579/?st=gallery.

Cartwright, Mark. "Hundred Years' War." *World History Encyclopedia*, March 17, 2020. https://www.worldhistory.org/Hundred_Years'_War/.

Castor, Helen. "Joan of Arc – Feminist Icon?" *The Guardian*, October 17, 2014. https://www.theguardian.com/books/2014/oct/17/joan-arc-feminist-icon-uncomfortable-fit.

Centre des Monuments Nationux (CMN). "History of Reims Cathedral." Accessed July 5, 2024. https://www.cathedrale-reims.fr/en/discover/.

Dalí, Salvador. *Joan of Arc*, 1977. Artnet. https://www.artnet.com/artists/salvador-dalí/joan-of-arc-kpPpPPEG2O3pKR5v3vuB6Q2.

De Pizan, Christine. *Ditié de Jeanne d'Arc*, ed. Angus J. Kennedy and Kennedy Varty (Oxford: Society for the Study of Medieval Languages and Literature 1977), trans. Leah Shopkow. https://dmdhist.sitehost.iu.edu/joan.htm.

"French Far-Right Monarchists Rally after Court Approves Joan of Arc Tribute." *RFI*, May 14, 2023. https://www.rfi.fr/en/france/20230514-french-far-right-monarchists-rally-after-court-gives-approval-for-joan-of-arc-commemoration.

Frohlick, Virginia. "Arrival at Chinon and the Trial at Poitiers" from *Saint Joan of Arc's Trial of Nullification*. The Saint Joan of Arc Center. Accessed July 3, 2024. http://www.stjoan-center.com/Trials/null05.html.

Green, David. "7 Facts about the Hundred Years' War." *History Extra*, July 17, 2018. https://www.historyextra.com/period/medieval/7-facts-about-the-hundred-years-war/.

Gregory, Philippa. "Joan of Arc Declared Innocent." *Philippa Gregory* (blog), July 7, 2018. https://www.philippagregory.com/news/joan-of-arc-declared-innocent.

Halsall, Paul. "Medieval Sourcebook: Joan of Arc: Letter to the King of England, 1429." In *Internet Medieval Sourcebook*, Paul Halsall/Fordham University, November 1996. https://sourcebooks.fordham.edu/source/joanofarc.asp.

Halsall, Paul. "Medieval Sourcebook: The Trial of Joan of Arc." In Internet Medieval Sourcebook, Paul Halsall/Fordham University, September 1999. https://sourcebooks.fordham.edu/basis/joanofarc-trial.asp.

Hickman, Kennedy. "Hundred Years' War: Battle of Patay." *ThoughtCo*, updated March 6, 2017. https://www.thoughtco.com/hundred-years-war-battle-of-patay-2360756.

Hickman, Kennedy. "Hundred Years' War: Siege of Orléans." *ThoughtCo*, updated December 2019. https://www.thoughtco.com/hundred-years-war-siege-of-orleans-2360758.

Hollway, Don. "Joan of Arc and the Siege of Orleans." *Warfare History Network*, January 3, 2020. https://warfarehistorynetwork.com/joan-of-arc-siege-of-orleans/.

"Holroyd, Michael. "A Tragedy without Villains." *The Guardian*, July 14, 2007. https://www.theguardian.com/books/2007/jul/14/theatre.stage.

"How Joan of Arc Turned the Tide in the Hundred Years' War." *National Geographic*, April 13, 2017. https://www.nationalgeographic.com/history/history-magazine/article/joan-of-arc-warrior-heretic-saint-martyr.

"Its Great Characters: Joan of Arc." Forteresse de Chinon. Accessed July 5, 2024. https://forteressechinon.fr/en/discover-fortress/its-great-characters/joan-arc.

Johnson, Wayne. "Janvier's Pantograph." *Medalblog*, December 27, 2010. https://medalblog.wordpress.com/2010/12/27/janviers_pantograph/.

Jeanne, icône populaire." Historical Jeanne d'Arc. Accessed July 6, 2024.https://sites.ina.fr/historial-jeannedarc/focus/chapitre/5/medias.

Jin, Trevor. "What Steps Are in the Beatification and Canonization Process?" *We Dare To Say*, July 24, 2019. https://wedaretosay.com/what-steps-are-in-the-beatification-and-canonization-process/.

"Joan of Arc." *Early and Medieval Christian Heresy*, University of Oregon, 2015. https://blogs.uoregon.edu/rel424s15drreis/joan-of-arc-fast-facts-and-imagery/.

"Joan of Arc 1865." Peter Nahum at the Leicester Galleries. Accessed July 6, 2024.

https://www.leicestergalleries.com/browse-artwork-detail/MTQ3Nzg=.

"Joan of Arc Chapter 5 Imprisonment and Trial." *Maid of Heaven*. Accessed July 6, 2024.

http://www.maidofheaven.com/joanofarc_gower_imprisonment_trial.asp.

"Joan of Arc Festival." Destination Orléans Val de Loire. Accessed July 6, 2024. https://www.tourisme-orleansmetropole.com/en/visit-orleans-get-inspired/must-see-highlights/joan-arc-festival/.

Kanehl, Steven R. "Jehanne La Pucelle: A mini biography." St. Joan of Arc Center. Accessed July 5, 2024. http://www.stjoan-center.com/time_line/part05.html.

Kennedy, Ben D. "Joan of Arc Chapter 5 Imprisonment and Trial." Maid of Heaven Foundation. Accessed June 29, 2024. http://www.maidofheaven.com/joanofarc_gower_imprisonment_trial.asp.

Kennedy, Ben D. "Joan of Arc & Charles VII: First Meeting." Maid of Heaven Foundation. Accessed July 5, 2024. http://www.maidofheaven.com/joanofarc_charlesvii_firstmeet.asp.

Kennedy, Ben D. "Trial of Nullification (Rehabilitation) Vacouleurs and the Journey to Chinon." Maid of Heaven Foundation. Accessed July 5, 2024. www.maidofheaven.com/joanofarc_nullification_vaucouleurs_chinon.asp.

Klemond, Susan. "At Her Trial, St. Joan of Arc Faced Her Accusers Alone." *National Catholic Register*, February 11, 2021. https://www.ncregister.com/blog/st-joan-of-arc-at-her-trial.

Lanhers, Yvonne. and Vale, Malcolm G.A. "St. Joan of Arc." *Encyclopedia Britannica*. July 22, 2024. https://www.britannica.com/biography/Saint-Joan-of-Arc/Capture-trial-and-execution.

Larcher, Theo. "Far-Right Supporters March in Paris to Mark 'Joan of Arc' Day." *The Connexion*, May 15, 2023.
https://www.connexionfrance.com/news/far-right-supporters-march-in-paris-to-mark-joan-of-arc-day/267299.

"Les Fêtes Johanniques 2024." Reims.fr. Accessed July 6, 2024. https://www.reims.fr/la-ville-de-reims/festivals-et-evenements/les-fetes-johanniques.

Lewis, Helen. "What If Joan of Arc Wasn't a Woman?" *The Atlantic*, September 2, 2022. https://www.theatlantic.com/ideas/archive/2022/09/joan-of-arc-nonbinary-globe/671321/.

Linder, Douglas O. "Deliberations, Final Trial Session, and Sentence (May 9-23, 1431)." UMKC School of Law: Famous Trials. Accessed June 30, 2024. https://www.famous-trials.com/the-trial-of-joan-of-arc-1431/2371-deliberations-final-trial-session-and-sentence-may-9-23-1431.

Luft, Laurent, Charles VII." Paris Historical Walks, December 12, 2013. http://paris-historic-walks.blogspot.com/2013/12/charles-vii.html.

Moorhouse, Dan. "Yolande of Aragon." The Hundred Years' War, February 22, 2022. https://thehundredyearswar.co.uk/yolande-of-aragon/

Murray, T. Douglas. "Sentence of Death." In *Jeanne d'Arc*, edited by Leah Shopko. McClure, Phillips, & Co., 1992. https://dmdhist.sitehost.iu.edu/joantrials.html#execution.

Phillips, James, et al. "Undiagnosing St Joan: She Does Not Need a Medical or Psychiatric Diagnosis." *Journal of Nervous and Mental Disease* 211, no. 8 (August 2023): 559–65. https://doi.org/10.1097/NMD.0000000000001654.

"Portraits of a Saint: Her Journey." Saint Joan of Arc.com. Accessed July 5, 2024. https://saint-joan-of-arc.com/journey.htm.

Powell, Nicole. "Joan of Arc Saved France." *World War I Poster Project*, 2014. https://cupola.gettysburg.edu/wwiposters/1.

Pronechen, Joseph. "The Step-by-Step Guide to How a Person Becomes a Canonized Saint." *National Catholic Register*, May 28, 2021. https://www.ncregister.com/blog/how-does-a-person-become-a-canonized-saint.

"Saints." United States Conference of Catholic Bishops. Accessed July 6, 2024. https://www.usccb.org/offices/public-affairs/saints.

Schildkrout, Barbara. "Joan of Arc–Hearing Voices." *American Journal of Psychiatry* 174, no. 12 (December 2017): 1153–54. https://doi.org/10.1176/appi.ajp.2017.17080948.

Shorr, Victoria. "What Joan of Arc Would Have Known about #MeToo." *Salon*, March 9, 2019. https://www.salon.com/2019/03/09/what-joan-of-arc-would-have-known-about-metoo/.

"*Sight & Sound Poll* 2012: *The Passion of Joan of Arc.*" Criterion Collection, September 18, 2012. https://www.criterion.com/current/posts/2475-sight-sound-poll-2012-the-passion-of-joan-of-ar.

Strauss, Matthew. "David Byrne Wrote a Musical About Joan of Arc." *Pitchfork*, May 19, 2016. pitchfork.com/news/65596-david-byrne-wrote-a-musical-about-joan-of-arc/.

"Study Guide 2007: *Saint Joan* by Bernard Shaw." Shaw Festival. Accessed July 6, 2024. https://www.shawfest.com/assets/guides/Saint_Joan_Study_Guide.pdf.

Tadié, Solène. "Joan of Arc, Saint of the Eternal." *National Catholic Register*, May 18, 2020. https://www.ncregister.com/features/joan-of-arc-saint-of-the-eternal.

"The Canonization Process: How Does The Church Declare A Saint?" *Diocesan*, August 1, 2016. https://diocesan.com/canonization-process-church-declare-saint/.

"Tower of Joan of Arc." Atlas Obscura. Accessed July 6, 2024. http://www.atlasobscura.com/places/tower-of-joan-of-arc-tour-jeanne-darc.

Twain, Mark. *Personal Recollections of Joan of Arc, by the Sieur Louis de Conte*. Harper & Brothers, 1896.

Wells, Jack; Bryan, Alfred; and Weston, Willie. "Joan of Arc They Are Calling You." Digital Commons at Connecticut College Historic Sheet Music Collection, 1917. https://digitalcommons.conncoll.edu/sheetmusic/777.

Welsh, William. "Joan of Arc's Loire Campaign: The English Tide Recedes," *Military Heritage* 14, no. 3 (2012), *Warfare History Network*. https://warfarehistorynetwork.com/article/joan-of-arc-and-the-loire-campaign-the-english-tide-recedes/.

"What were the miracles that the Vatican accepted raise Joan of Arc to the official rank of Canonized Saint?" The Saint Joan of Arc Center. Accessed July 6, 2024. http://www.stjoan-center.com/FAQ/question7.html.

Williamson, Allen. Segment 8: The March to Reims." Joan of Arc Archive. Accessed July 5, 2024. https://joan-of-arc.org/joanofarc_life_summary_rheims.html

"Women Prophets and Visionaries in France at the End of the Middle Ages." *Women in World History: A Biographical Encyclopedia*. Enyclopedia.com, September 11, 2024. https://www.encyclopedia.com/women/encyclopedias-almanacs-transcripts-and-maps/women-prophets-and-visionaries-france-end-middle-ages.

Image Sources

[1] *Goran tek-en, CC BY-SA 4.0 <https://creativecommons.org/licenses/by-sa/4.0>, via Wikimedia Commons; https://commons.wikimedia.org/wiki/File:Guyenne_1328-en.svg*

[2] *Jules Bastien-Lepage, CC0, via Wikimedia Commons; https://commons.wikimedia.org/wiki/File:Joan_of_Arc_MET_DP-14201-049.jpg*

[3] *https://commons.wikimedia.org/wiki/File:Yolande_Aragon_Vierge_Enfant.jpg*

[4] *https://commons.wikimedia.org/wiki/File:Jeanne_d%27Arc_pr%C3%A9sent%C3%A9e_%C3%A0_Charles_VII_(cropped).jpg*

[5] *https://commons.wikimedia.org/wiki/File:Joan_of_Arc_miniature_graded.jpg*

[6] *https://commons.wikimedia.org/wiki/File:Contemporaine_afb_jeanne_d_arc.png*

[7] *https://commons.wikimedia.org/wiki/File:View_of_Orl%C3%A9ans_1428_-_Project_Gutenberg_etext_19488.jpg*

[8] *https://commons.wikimedia.org/wiki/File:Battle_of_Herrings.jpg*

[9] *https://commons.wikimedia.org/wiki/File:Scherrer_jeanne_enters_orlean.jpg*

[10] *https://commons.wikimedia.org/wiki/File:Lenepveu,_Jeanne_d%27Arc_au_si%C3%A8ge_d%27Orl%C3%A9ans.jpg*

[11] *https://commons.wikimedia.org/wiki/File:Ingres_coronation_charles_vii.jpg*

[12] *Fab5669, CC BY-SA 3.0 <https://creativecommons.org/licenses/by-sa/3.0>, via Wikimedia Commons; https://commons.wikimedia.org/wiki/File:Reims_-_plaque_Jeanne_d%27Arc.JPG*

[13] *https://commons.wikimedia.org/wiki/File:Vigiles_du_roi_Charles_VII_05.jpeg*

[14] *https://commons.wikimedia.org/wiki/File:Panth%C3%A9on_-_La_vie_de_Jeanne_d%27Arc_(hlw16_0310)-_crop_capture_(cropped).jpg*

[15] *https://commons.wikimedia.org/wiki/File:Pierre_Cauchon-Jeanne_Darc_manuscript.jpg*

[16] https://en.wikipedia.org/wiki/File:Joan_of_Arc_Canonization.jpg

[17] https://commons.wikimedia.org/wiki/File:Joan_of_Arc_WWI_lithograph.jpg
[18] https://commons.wikimedia.org/wiki/File:The_Passion_of_Joan_of_Arc_(1928)_English_Poster.png
[19] https://commons.wikimedia.org/wiki/File:Saintjoanposter1957.JPG
[20] https://commons.wikimedia.org/wiki/File:Jeanne_d%27Arc,_atelier_Rubens.jpg
[21] https://commons.wikimedia.org/wiki/File:Joan_of_Arc_-_John_Everett_Millais.jpg
[22] https://commons.wikimedia.org/wiki/File:Craig_Franck_joan_ark.jpeg

www.ingramcontent.com/pod-product-compliance
Lightning Source LLC
Chambersburg PA
CBHW070339010526
44107CB00004B/560